FREE Test Taking Tips DVD Offer

To help us better serve you, we have developed a Test Taking Tips DVD that we would like to give you for FREE. **This DVD covers world-class test taking tips that you can use to be even more successful when you are taking your test.**

All that we ask is that you email us your feedback about your study guide. Please let us know what you thought about it – whether that is good, bad or indifferent.

To get your **FREE Test Taking Tips DVD**, email freedvd@studyguideteam.com with "FREE DVD" in the subject line and the following information in the body of the email:

a. The title of your study guide.

b. Your product rating on a scale of 1-5, with 5 being the highest rating.

c. Your feedback about the study guide. What did you think of it?

d. Your full name and shipping address to send your free DVD.

If you have any questions or concerns, please don't hesitate to contact us at freedvd@studyguideteam.com.

Thanks again!

Next-Generation ACCUPLACER Study Guide

Test Prep & Practice Test Questions for the Next-Generation ACCUPLACER Exam

Test Prep Books College Placement Prep Team

Table of Contents

Quick Overview

As you draw closer to taking your exam, effective preparation becomes more and more important. Thankfully, you have this study guide to help you get ready. Use this guide to help keep your studying on track and refer to it often.

This study guide contains several key sections that will help you be successful on your exam. The guide contains tips for what you should do the night before and the day of the test. Also included are test-taking tips. Knowing the right information is not always enough. Many well-prepared test takers struggle with exams. These tips will help equip you to accurately read, assess, and answer test questions.

A large part of the guide is devoted to showing you what content to expect on the exam and to helping you better understand that content. Near the end of this guide is a practice test so that you can see how well you have grasped the content. Then, answer explanations are provided so that you can understand why you missed certain questions.

Don't try to cram the night before you take your exam. This is not a wise strategy for a few reasons. First, your retention of the information will be low. Your time would be better used by reviewing information you already know rather than trying to learn a lot of new information. Second, you will likely become stressed as you try to gain a large amount of knowledge in a short amount of time. Third, you will be depriving yourself of sleep. So be sure to go to bed at a reasonable time the night before. Being well-rested helps you focus and remain calm.

Be sure to eat a substantial breakfast the morning of the exam. If you are taking the exam in the afternoon, be sure to have a good lunch as well. Being hungry is distracting and can make it difficult to focus. You have hopefully spent lots of time preparing for the exam. Don't let an empty stomach get in the way of success!

When travelling to the testing center, leave earlier than needed. That way, you have a buffer in case you experience any delays. This will help you remain calm and will keep you from missing your appointment time at the testing center.

Be sure to pace yourself during the exam. Don't try to rush through the exam. There is no need to risk performing poorly on the exam just so you can leave the testing center early. Allow yourself to use all of the allotted time if needed.

Remain positive while taking the exam even if you feel like you are performing poorly. Thinking about the content you should have mastered will not help you perform better on the exam.

Once the exam is complete, take some time to relax. Even if you feel that you need to take the exam again, you will be well served by some down time before you begin studying again. It's often easier to convince yourself to study if you know that it will come with a reward!

Test-Taking Strategies

1. Predicting the Answer

When you feel confident in your preparation for a multiple-choice test, try predicting the answer before reading the answer choices. This is especially useful on questions that test objective factual knowledge or that ask you to fill in a blank. By predicting the answer before reading the available choices, you eliminate the possibility that you will be distracted or led astray by an incorrect answer choice. You will feel more confident in your selection if you read the question, predict the answer, and then find your prediction among the answer choices. After using this strategy, be sure to still read all of the answer choices carefully and completely. If you feel unprepared, you should not attempt to predict the answers. This would be a waste of time and an opportunity for your mind to wander in the wrong direction.

2. Reading the Whole Question

Too often, test takers scan a multiple-choice question, recognize a few familiar words, and immediately jump to the answer choices. Test authors are aware of this common impatience, and they will sometimes prey upon it. For instance, a test author might subtly turn the question into a negative, or he or she might redirect the focus of the question right at the end. The only way to avoid falling into these traps is to read the entirety of the question carefully before reading the answer choices.

3. Looking for Wrong Answers

Long and complicated multiple-choice questions can be intimidating. One way to simplify a difficult multiple-choice question is to eliminate all of the answer choices that are clearly wrong. In most sets of answers, there will be at least one selection that can be dismissed right away. If the test is administered on paper, the test taker could draw a line through it to indicate that it may be ignored; otherwise, the test taker will have to perform this operation mentally or on scratch paper. In either case, once the obviously incorrect answers have been eliminated, the remaining choices may be considered. Sometimes identifying the clearly wrong answers will give the test taker some information about the correct answer. For instance, if one of the remaining answer choices is a direct opposite of one of the eliminated answer choices, it may well be the correct answer. The opposite of obviously wrong is obviously right! Of course, this is not always the case. Some answers are obviously incorrect simply because they are irrelevant to the question being asked. Still, identifying and eliminating some incorrect answer choices is a good way to simplify a multiple-choice question.

4. Don't Overanalyze

Anxious test takers often overanalyze questions. When you are nervous, your brain will often run wild, causing you to make associations and discover clues that don't actually exist. If you feel that this may be a problem for you, do whatever you can to slow down during the test. Try taking a deep breath or counting to ten. As you read and consider the question, restrict yourself to the particular words used by the author. Avoid thought tangents about what the author *really* meant, or what he or she was *trying* to say. The only things that matter on a multiple-choice test are the words that are actually in the question. You must avoid reading too much into a multiple-choice question, or supposing that the writer meant something other than what he or she wrote.

5. No Need for Panic

It is wise to learn as many strategies as possible before taking a multiple-choice test, but it is likely that you will come across a few questions for which you simply don't know the answer. In this situation, avoid panicking. Because most multiple-choice tests include dozens of questions, the relative value of a single wrong answer is small. Moreover, your failure on one question has no effect on your success elsewhere on the test. As much as possible, you should compartmentalize each question on a multiple-choice test. In other words, you should not allow your feelings about one question to affect your success on the others. When you find a question that you either don't understand or don't know how to answer, just take a deep breath and do your best. Read the entire question slowly and carefully. Try rephrasing the question a couple of different ways. Then, read all of the answer choices carefully. After eliminating obviously wrong answers, make a selection and move on to the next question.

6. Confusing Answer Choices

When working on a difficult multiple-choice question, there may be a tendency to focus on the answer choices that are the easiest to understand. Many people, whether consciously or not, gravitate to the answer choices that require the least concentration, knowledge, and memory. This is a mistake. When you come across an answer choice that is confusing, you should give it extra attention. A question might be confusing because you do not know the subject matter to which it refers. If this is the case, don't eliminate the answer before you have affirmatively settled on another. When you come across an answer choice of this type, set it aside as you look at the remaining choices. If you can confidently assert that one of the other choices is correct, you can leave the confusing answer aside. Otherwise, you will need to take a moment to try to better understand the confusing answer choice. Rephrasing is one way to tease out the sense of a confusing answer choice.

7. Your First Instinct

Many people struggle with multiple-choice tests because they overthink the questions. If you have studied sufficiently for the test, you should be prepared to trust your first instinct once you have carefully and completely read the question and all of the answer choices. There is a great deal of research suggesting that the mind can come to the correct conclusion very quickly once it has obtained all of the relevant information. At times, it may seem to you as if your intuition is working faster even than your reasoning mind. This may in fact be true. The knowledge you obtain while studying may be retrieved from your subconscious before you have a chance to work out the associations that support it. Verify your instinct by working out the reasons that it should be trusted.

8. Key Words

Many test takers struggle with multiple-choice questions because they have poor reading comprehension skills. Quickly reading and understanding a multiple-choice question requires a mixture of skill and experience. To help with this, try jotting down a few key words and phrases on a piece of scrap paper. Doing this concentrates the process of reading and forces the mind to weigh the relative importance of the question's parts. In selecting words and phrases to write down, the test taker thinks about the question more deeply and carefully. This is especially true for multiple-choice questions that are preceded by a long prompt.

9. Subtle Negatives

One of the oldest tricks in the multiple-choice test writer's book is to subtly reverse the meaning of a question with a word like *not* or *except*. If you are not paying attention to each word in the question, you can easily be led astray by this trick. For instance, a common question format is, "Which of the following is...?" Obviously, if the question instead is, "Which of the following is not...?," then the answer will be quite different. Even worse, the test makers are aware of the potential for this mistake and will include one answer choice that would be correct if the question were not negated or reversed. A test taker who misses the reversal will find what he or she believes to be a correct answer and will be so confident that he or she will fail to reread the question and discover the original error. The only way to avoid this is to practice a wide variety of multiple-choice questions and to pay close attention to each and every word.

10. Reading Every Answer Choice

It may seem obvious, but you should always read every one of the answer choices! Too many test takers fall into the habit of scanning the question and assuming that they understand the question because they recognize a few key words. From there, they pick the first answer choice that answers the question they believe they have read. Test takers who read all of the answer choices might discover that one of the latter answer choices is actually *more* correct. Moreover, reading all of the answer choices can remind you of facts related to the question that can help you arrive at the correct answer. Sometimes, a misstatement or incorrect detail in one of the latter answer choices will trigger your memory of the subject and will enable you to find the right answer. Failing to read all of the answer choices is like not reading all of the items on a restaurant menu: you might miss out on the perfect choice.

11. Spot the Hedges

One of the keys to success on multiple-choice tests is paying close attention to every word. This is never more true than with words like *almost, most, some,* and *sometimes*. These words are called "hedges" because they indicate that a statement is not totally true or not true in every place and time. An absolute statement will contain no hedges, but in many subjects, like literature and history, the answers are not always straightforward or absolute. There are always exceptions to the rules in these subjects. For this reason, you should favor those multiple-choice questions that contain hedging language. The presence of qualifying words indicates that the author is taking special care with his or her words, which is certainly important when composing the right answer. After all, there are many ways to be wrong, but there is only one way to be right! For this reason, it is wise to avoid answers that are absolute when taking a multiple-choice test. An absolute answer is one that says things are either all one way or all another. They often include words like *every, always, best,* and *never*. If you are taking a multiple-choice test in a subject that doesn't lend itself to absolute answers, be on your guard if you see any of these words.

12. Long Answers

In many subject areas, the answers are not simple. As already mentioned, the right answer often requires hedges. Another common feature of the answers to a complex or subjective question are qualifying clauses, which are groups of words that subtly modify the meaning of the sentence. If the question or answer choice describes a rule to which there are exceptions or the subject matter is complicated, ambiguous, or confusing, the correct answer will require many words in order to be expressed clearly and accurately. In essence, you should not be deterred by answer choices that seem excessively long. Oftentimes, the author of the text will not be able to write the correct answer without offering some qualifications and modifications. Your job is to read the answer choices thoroughly and completely and to select the one that most accurately and precisely answers the question.

13. Restating to Understand

Sometimes, a question on a multiple-choice test is difficult not because of what it asks but because of how it is written. If this is the case, restate the question or answer choice in different words. This process serves a couple of important purposes. First, it forces you to concentrate on the core of the question. In order to rephrase the question accurately, you have to understand it well. Rephrasing the question will concentrate your mind on the key words and ideas. Second, it will present the information to your mind in a fresh way. This process may trigger your memory and render some useful scrap of information picked up while studying.

14. True Statements

Sometimes an answer choice will be true in itself, but it does not answer the question. This is one of the main reasons why it is essential to read the question carefully and completely before proceeding to the answer choices. Too often, test takers skip ahead to the answer choices and look for true statements. Having found one of these, they are content to select it without reference to the question above. Obviously, this provides an easy way for test makers to play tricks. The savvy test taker will always read the entire question before turning to the answer choices. Then, having settled on a correct answer choice, he or she will refer to the original question and ensure that the selected answer is relevant. The mistake of choosing a correct-but-irrelevant answer choice is especially common on questions related to specific pieces of objective knowledge, like historical or scientific facts. A prepared test taker will have a wealth of factual knowledge at his or her disposal, and should not be careless in its application.

15. No Patterns

One of the more dangerous ideas that circulates about multiple-choice tests is that the correct answers tend to fall into patterns. These erroneous ideas range from a belief that B and C are the most common right answers, to the idea that an unprepared test-taker should answer "A-B-A-C-A-D-A-B-A." It cannot be emphasized enough that pattern-seeking of this type is exactly the WRONG way to approach a multiple-choice test. To begin with, it is highly unlikely that the test maker will plot the correct answers according to some predetermined pattern. The questions are scrambled and delivered in a random order. Furthermore, even if the test maker was following a pattern in the assignation of correct answers, there is no reason why the test taker would know which pattern he or she was using. Any attempt to discern a pattern in the answer choices is a waste of time and a distraction from the real work of taking the test. A test taker would be much better served by extra preparation before the test than by reliance on a pattern in the answers.

FREE DVD OFFER

Don't forget that doing well on your exam includes both understanding the test content and understanding how to use what you know to do well on the test. We offer a completely FREE Test Taking Tips DVD that covers world class test taking tips that you can use to be even more successful when you are taking your test.

All that we ask is that you email us your feedback about your study guide. To get your **FREE Test Taking Tips DVD**, email freedvd@studyguideteam.com with "FREE DVD" in the subject line and the following information in the body of the email:

- The title of your study guide.
- Your product rating on a scale of 1-5, with 5 being the highest rating.
- Your feedback about the study guide. What did you think of it?
- Your full name and shipping address to send your free DVD.

Introduction to the Next-Generation ACCUPLACER

Function of the Test

The Next-Generation ACCUPLACER is an adaptive, computerized test offered by the College Board and used by some colleges and high schools to determine placement of students in programs appropriate to the students' skill level. This test has redesigned reading, writing, and math content. This test was redesigned from the ACCUPLACER to better align with the content domain continuum of the SAT Suite of Assessments. The Next-Generation ACCUPLACER will also help institutions improve course placement accuracy. The test is offered nation-wide, at any college or high school that chooses to use it. Test-takers are almost always students of schools that use the Next-Generation ACCUPLACER in their course selection and placement efforts. Schools can also use the Next-Generation ACCUPLACER to assess students' skill levels and identify specific areas in which the students need improvement. Scores are generally used only by the college or high school the student is already attending for placement and instruction at that school.

Test Administration

The Next-Generation ACCUPLACER is a computer-adaptive test. This means that the computer will draw from a pool of questions written to the test specifications that represent a range of difficulty. The questions themselves and the sequence in which they are delivered will vary from student to student. The test uses a complex question-selection algorithm based on a weighted deviations model. If a student answers a question correctly then the next question will be slightly more difficult. If the question is answered incorrectly then the next question will be slightly easier.

Fees for taking the ACCUPLACER vary from school to school. Students sometimes do not pay a fee at all; rather, the school pays the College Board for the right to administer the test and then students take it for free. Students may retake the ACCUPLACER at the discretion of the school administering the test and using its results. Students with documented disabilities can make arrangements, through the test center offering the ACCUPLACER, to take the test with appropriate accommodations, including the potential availability of a written version of the test.

Test Format

The core of the Next-Generation ACCUPLACER is five multiple-choice subject area tests: Reading, Writing, Arithmetic, Quantitative Reasoning, Algebra and Statistics (QAS), and Advanced Algebra and Functions (AAF). A college may ask a student to test in any or all of the five subject areas, depending on the student's and the school's needs.

There is no time-limit, so test takers should feel free to work at their own pace. A typical test section might take around 30 minutes to complete as there are 20 questions per section.

Section	Questions
Reading	20
Writing	20
Arithmetic	20
Quantitative Reasoning, Algebra, and Statistics	20
Advanced Algebra and Functions	20

Scoring

The College Board will provide a concordance for each of the corresponding tests to help students compare scores from the classic assessments to the next-generation assessments. Schools are free to use the scores for placement as they see fit, given that the difficulty of coursework varies from school to school. Scores are typically generated instantly by the computer but may not be available from the school administering the test until the school has had a chance to review the scores and use them for placement purposes.

Recent/Future Developments

The Next-Generation ACCUPLACER is the latest update to the ACCUPLACER placement tests.

Reading

Information and Ideas

Topic Versus the Main Idea

It is very important to know the difference between the topic and the main idea of the text. Even though these two are similar because they both present the central point of a text, they have distinctive differences. A *topic* is the subject of the text; it can usually be described in a one- to two-word phrase and appears in the simplest form. On the other hand, the *main idea* is more detailed and provides the author's central point of the text. It can be expressed through a complete sentence and can be found in the beginning, middle, or end of a paragraph. In most nonfiction books, the first sentence of the passage usually (but not always) states the main idea. Take a look at the passage below to review the topic versus the main idea.

Cheetahs

> Cheetahs are one of the fastest mammals on land, reaching up to 70 miles an hour over short distances. Even though cheetahs can run as fast as 70 miles an hour, they usually only have to run half that speed to catch up with their choice of prey. Cheetahs cannot maintain a fast pace over long periods of time because they will overheat their bodies. After a chase, cheetahs need to rest for approximately 30 minutes prior to eating or returning to any other activity.

In the example above, the topic of the passage is "Cheetahs" simply because that is the subject of the text. The main idea of the text is "Cheetahs are one of the fastest mammals on land but can only maintain this fast pace for short distances." While it covers the topic, it is more detailed and refers to the text in its entirety. The text continues to provide additional details called *supporting details,* which will be discussed in the next section.

Supporting Details

Supporting details help readers better develop and understand the main idea. Supporting details answer questions like *who, what, where, when, why,* and *how*. Different types of supporting details include examples, facts and statistics, anecdotes, and sensory details.

Persuasive and informative texts often use supporting details. In persuasive texts, authors attempt to make readers agree with their point of view, and supporting details are often used as "selling points." If authors make a statement, they should support the statement with evidence in order to adequately persuade readers. Informative texts use supporting details such as examples and facts to inform readers. Take another look at the previous "Cheetahs" passage to find examples of supporting details.

Cheetahs

> Cheetahs are one of the fastest mammals on land, reaching up to 70 miles an hour over short distances. Even though cheetahs can run as fast as 70 miles an hour, they usually only have to run half that speed to catch up with their choice of prey. Cheetahs cannot maintain a fast pace over long periods of time because they will overheat their bodies. After a chase, cheetahs need to rest for approximately 30 minutes prior to eating or returning to any other activity.

In the example above, supporting details include:

- Cheetahs reach up to 70 miles per hour over short distances.
- They usually only have to run half that speed to catch up with their prey.
- Cheetahs will overheat their bodies if they exert a high speed over longer distances.
- Cheetahs need to rest for 30 minutes after a chase.

Look at the diagram below (applying the cheetah example) to help determine the hierarchy of topic, main idea, and supporting details.

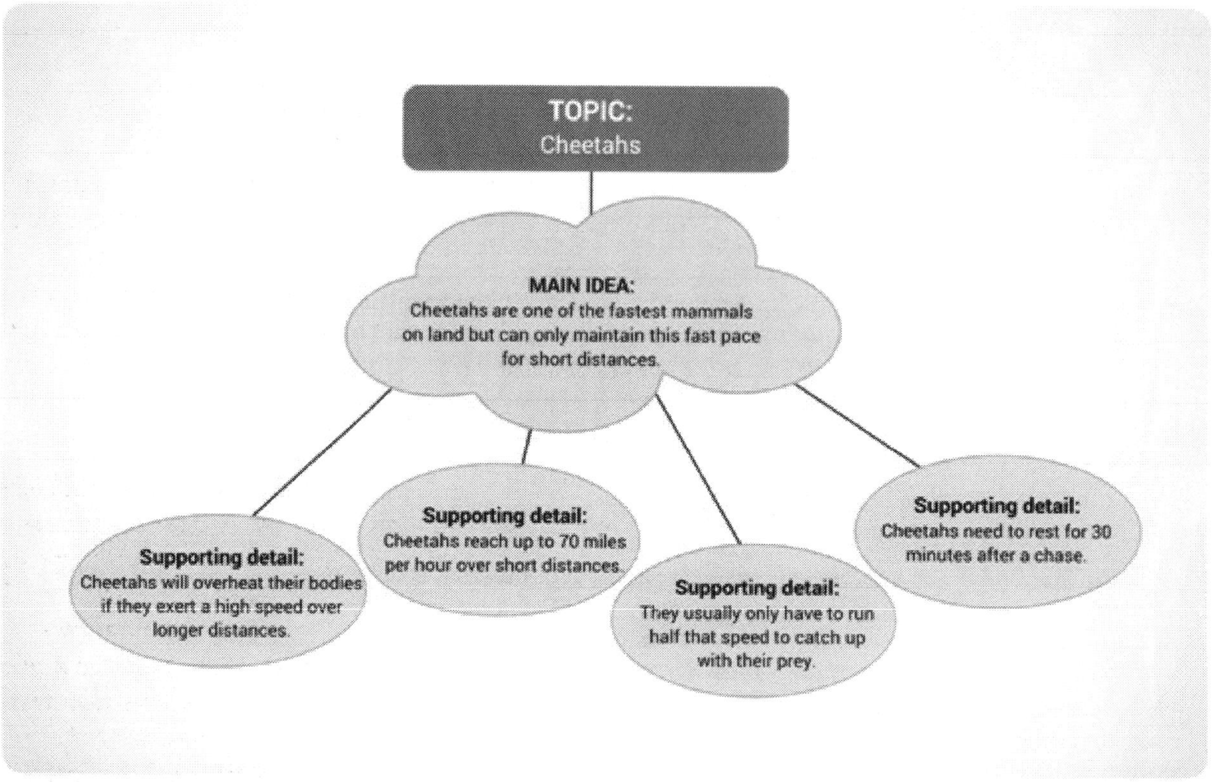

Drawing Conclusions

When drawing conclusions about texts or passages, readers should do two main things: 1) Use the information that they already know and 2) Use the information they have learned from the text or passage. Authors write with an intended purpose, and it is the reader's responsibility to understand and form logical conclusions of authors' ideas. It is important to remember that the reader's conclusions should be supported by information directly from the text. Readers cannot simply form conclusions based off of only information they already know.

There are several ways readers can draw conclusions from authors' ideas, such as note taking, text evidence, text credibility, writing a response to text, directly stated information versus implications, outlining, summarizing, and paraphrasing. Let's take a look at each important strategy to help readers draw logical conclusions.

Note Taking

When readers take notes throughout texts or passages, they are jotting down important facts or points that the author makes. Note taking is a useful record of information that helps readers understand the text or passage and respond to it. When taking notes, readers should keep lines brief and filled with pertinent information so that they are not rereading a large amount of text, but rather just key points, elements, or words. After readers have completed a text or passage, they can refer to their notes to help them form a conclusion about the author's ideas in the text or passage.

Text Evidence

Text evidence is the information readers find in a text or passage that supports the main idea or point(s) in a story. In turn, text evidence can help readers draw conclusions about the text or passage. The information should be taken directly from the text or passage and placed in quotation marks. Text evidence provides readers with information to support ideas about the text so that they do not rely simply on their own thoughts. Details should be precise, descriptive, and factual. Statistics are a great piece of text evidence because they provide readers with exact numbers and not just a generalization. For example, instead of saying "Asia has a larger population than Europe," authors could provide detailed information such as, "In Asia there are over 4 billion people, whereas in Europe there are a little over 750 million." More definitive information provides better evidence to readers to help support their conclusions about texts or passages.

Text Credibility

Credible sources are important when drawing conclusions because readers need to be able to trust what they are reading. Authors should always use credible sources to help gain the trust of their readers. A text is *credible* when it is believable and the author is objective and unbiased. If readers do not trust an author's words, they may simply dismiss the text completely. For example, if an author writes a persuasive essay, he or she is outwardly trying to sway readers' opinions to align with his or her own. Readers may agree or disagree with the author, which may, in turn, lead them to believe that the author is credible or not credible. Also, readers should keep in mind the source of the text. If readers review a journal about astronomy, would a more reliable source be a NASA employee or a medical doctor? Overall, text credibility is important when drawing conclusions, because readers want reliable sources that support the decisions they have made about the author's ideas.

Writing a Response to Text

Once readers have determined their opinions and validated the credibility of a text, they can then reflect on the text. Writing a response to a text is one way readers can reflect on the given text or passage. When readers write responses to a text, it is important for them to rely on the evidence within the text to support their opinions or thoughts. Supporting evidence such as facts, details, statistics, and quotes directly from the text are key pieces of information readers should reflect upon or use when writing a response to text.

Directly Stated Information Versus Implications

Engaged readers should constantly self-question while reviewing texts to help them form conclusions. Self-questioning is when readers review a paragraph, page, passage, or chapter and ask themselves, "Did I understand what I read?," "What was the main event in this section?," "Where is this taking place?," and so on. Authors can provide clues or pieces of evidence throughout a text or passage to guide readers toward a conclusion. This is why active and engaged readers should read the text or passage in its entirety before forming a definitive conclusion. If readers do not gather all the pieces of evidence needed, then they may jump to an illogical conclusion.

At times, authors directly state conclusions while others simply imply them. Of course, it is easier if authors outwardly provide conclusions to readers because it does not leave any information open to interpretation. On the other hand, implications are things that authors do not directly state but can be assumed based off of information they provided. If authors only imply what may have happened, readers can form a menagerie of ideas for conclusions. For example, look at the following statement: "Once we heard the sirens, we hunkered down in the storm shelter." In this statement, the author does not directly state that there was a tornado, but clues such as "sirens" and "storm shelter" provide insight to the readers to help form that conclusion.

Outlining

An outline is a system used to organize writing. When reading texts, outlining is important because it helps readers organize important information in a logical pattern using roman numerals. Usually, outlines start with the main idea(s) and then branch out into subgroups or subsidiary thoughts of subjects. Not only do outlines provide a visual tool for readers to reflect on how events, characters, settings, or other key parts of the text or passage relate to one another, but they can also lead readers to a stronger conclusion.

The sample below demonstrates what a general outline looks like.

I. Main Topic 1
   a. Subtopic 1
   b. Subtopic 2
      1. Detail 1
      2. Detail 2
II. Main Topic 2
   a. Subtopic 1
   b. Subtopic 2
      1. Detail 1
      2. Detail 2

Summarizing

At the end of a text or passage, it is important to summarize what the readers read. Summarizing is a strategy in which readers determine what is important throughout the text or passage, shorten those ideas, and rewrite or retell it in their own words. A summary should identify the main idea of the text or passage. Important details or supportive evidence should also be accurately reported in the summary. If writers provide irrelevant details in the summary, it may cloud the greater meaning of the summary in the text. When summarizing, writers should not include their opinions, quotes, or what they thought the author should have said. A clear summary provides clarity of the text or passage to the readers. Let's review the checklist of items writers should include in their summary.

Summary Checklist

- Title of the story
- Someone: Who is or are the main character(s)?
- Wanted: What did the character(s) want?
- But: What was the problem?
- So: How did the character(s) solve the problem?
- Then: How did the story end? What was the resolution?

Paraphrasing

Another strategy readers can use to help them fully comprehend a text or passage is paraphrasing. Paraphrasing is when readers take the author's words and put them into their own words. When readers and writers paraphrase, they should avoid copying the text—that is plagiarism. It is also important to include as many details as possible when restating the facts. Not only will this help readers and writers recall information, but by putting the information into their own words, they demonstrate whether or not they fully comprehend the text or passage. Look at the example below showing an original text and how to paraphrase it.

> *Original Text*: Fenway Park is home to the beloved Boston Red Sox. The stadium opened on April 20, 1912. The stadium currently seats over 37,000 fans, many of whom travel from all over the country to experience the iconic team and nostalgia of Fenway Park.
>
> *Paraphrased*: On April 20, 1912, Fenway Park opened. Home to the Boston Red Sox, the stadium now seats over 37,000 fans. Many spectators travel to watch the Red Sox and experience the spirit of Fenway Park.

Paraphrasing, summarizing, and quoting can often cross paths with one another. Review the chart below showing the similarities and differences between the three strategies.

Paraphrasing	Summarizing	Quoting
Uses own words	Puts main ideas into own words	Uses words that are identical to text
References original source	References original source	Requires quotation marks
Uses own sentences	Shows important ideas of source	Uses author's own words and ideas

Rhetoric

Authors utilize a wide range of techniques to tell a story or communicate information. Readers should be familiar with the most common of these techniques. Techniques of writing are also commonly known as rhetorical devices.

Types of Appeals

In non-fiction writing, authors employ argumentative techniques to present their opinion to readers in the most convincing way. First of all, persuasive writing usually includes at least one type of appeal: an appeal to logic (logos), emotion (pathos), or credibility and trustworthiness (ethos). When a writer appeals to logic, they are asking readers to agree with them based on research, evidence, and an established line of reasoning. An author's argument might also appeal to readers' emotions, perhaps by including personal stories and anecdotes (a short narrative of a specific event). A final type of appeal, appeal to authority, asks the reader to agree with the author's argument on the basis of their expertise or credentials. Consider three different approaches to arguing the same opinion:

Logic (Logos)
This is an example of an appeal to logic:

> Our school should abolish its current ban on cell phone use on campus. This rule was adopted last year as an attempt to reduce class disruptions and help students focus more on their lessons. However, since the rule was enacted, there has been no change in the number of disciplinary problems in class. Therefore, the rule is ineffective and should be done away with.

The author uses evidence to disprove the logic of the school's rule (the rule was supposed to reduce discipline problems; the number of problems has not been reduced; therefore, the rule is not working) and call for its repeal.

Emotion (Pathos)
An author's argument might also appeal to readers' emotions, perhaps by including personal stories and anecdotes. The next example presents an appeal to emotion. By sharing the personal anecdote of one student and speaking about emotional topics like family relationships, the author invokes the reader's empathy in asking them to reconsider the school rule.

> Our school should abolish its current ban on cell phone use on campus. If they aren't able to use their phones during the school day, many students feel isolated from their loved ones. For example, last semester, one student's grandmother had a heart attack in the morning. However, because he couldn't use his cell phone, the student didn't know about his grandmother's accident until the end of the day—when she had already passed away and it was too late to say goodbye. By preventing students from contacting their friends and family, our school is placing undue stress and anxiety on students.

Credibility (Ethos)
Finally, an appeal to authority includes a statement from a relevant expert. In this case, the author uses a doctor in the field of education to support the argument. All three examples begin from the same opinion—the school's phone ban needs to change—but rely on different argumentative styles to persuade the reader.

> Our school should abolish its current ban on cell phone use on campus. According to Dr. Bartholomew Everett, a leading educational expert, "Research studies show that cell phone usage has no real impact on student attentiveness. Rather, phones provide a valuable technological resource for learning. Schools need to learn how to integrate this new technology into their curriculum." Rather than banning phones altogether, our school should follow the advice of experts and allow students to use phones as part of their learning.

Rhetorical Questions

Another commonly used argumentative technique is asking rhetorical questions, questions that do not actually require an answer but that push the reader to consider the topic further.

> I wholly disagree with the proposal to ban restaurants from serving foods with high sugar and sodium contents. Do we really want to live in a world where the government can control what we eat? I prefer to make my own food choices.

Here, the author's rhetorical question prompts readers to put themselves in a hypothetical situation and imagine how they would feel about it.

Figurative Language

Literary texts also employ rhetorical devices. Figurative language like simile and metaphor is a type of rhetorical device commonly found in literature. In addition to rhetorical devices that play on the *meanings* of words, there are also rhetorical devices that use the *sounds* of words. These devices are most often found in poetry but may also be found in other types of literature and in non-fiction writing like speech texts.

Alliteration and *assonance* are both varieties of sound repetition. Other types of sound repetition include: anaphora, repetition that occurs at the beginning of the sentences; epiphora, repetition occurring at the end of phrases; antimetabole, repetition of words in reverse order; and antiphrasis, a form of denial of an assertion in a text.

Alliteration refers to the repetition of the first sound of each word. Recall Robert Burns' opening line:

> My love is like a red, red rose

This line includes two instances of alliteration: "love" and "like" (repeated *L* sound), as well as "red" and "rose" (repeated *R* sound). Next, assonance refers to the repetition of vowel sounds, and can occur anywhere within a word (not just the opening sound). Here is the opening of a poem by John Keats:

> When I have fears that I may cease to be
>
> Before my pen has glean'd my teeming brain

Assonance can be found in the words "fears," "cease," "be," "glean'd," and "teeming," all of which stress the long *E* sound. Both alliteration and assonance create a harmony that unifies the writer's language.

Another sound device is *onomatopoeia*, or words whose spelling mimics the sound they describe. Words like "crash," "bang," and "sizzle" are all examples of onomatopoeia. Use of onomatopoetic language adds auditory imagery to the text.

Readers are probably most familiar with the technique of *pun*. A pun is a play on words, taking advantage of two words that have the same or similar pronunciation. Puns can be found throughout Shakespeare's plays, for instance:

> Now is the winter of our discontent
> Made glorious summer by this son of York

These lines from *Richard III* contain a play on words. Richard III refers to his brother, the newly crowned King Edward IV, as the "son of York," referencing their family heritage from the house of York. However, while drawing a comparison between the political climate and the weather (times of political trouble were the "winter," but now the new king brings "glorious summer"), Richard's use of the word "son" also implies another word with the same pronunciation, "sun"—so Edward IV is also like the sun, bringing light, warmth, and hope to England. Puns are a clever way for writers to suggest two meanings at once.

Counterarguments

If an author presents a differing opinion or a counterargument in order to refute it, the reader should consider how and why this information is being presented. It is meant to strengthen the original argument and shouldn't be confused with the author's intended conclusion, but it should also be considered in the reader's final evaluation.

Authors can also use bias if they ignore the opposing viewpoint or present their side in an unbalanced way. A strong argument considers the opposition and finds a way to refute it. Critical readers should look for an unfair or one-sided presentation of the argument and be skeptical, as a bias may be present. Even if this bias is unintentional, if it exists in the writing, the reader should be wary of the validity of the argument. Readers should also look for the use of stereotypes, which refer to specific groups. Stereotypes are often negative connotations about a person or place, and should always be avoided. When a critical reader finds stereotypes in a piece of writing, they should be critical of the argument, and consider the validity of anything the author presents. Stereotypes reveal a flaw in the writer's thinking and may suggest a lack of knowledge or understanding about the subject.

Meaning of Words in Context

There will be many occasions in one's reading career in which an unknown word or a word with multiple meanings will pop up. There are ways of determining what these words or phrases mean that do not require the use of the dictionary, which is especially helpful during a test where one may not be available. Even outside of the exam, knowing how to derive an understanding of a word via context clues will be a critical skill in the real world. The context is the circumstances in which a story or a passage is happening, and can usually be found in the series of words directly before or directly after the word or phrase in question. The clues are the words that hint towards the meaning of the unknown word or phrase.

There may be questions that ask about the meaning of a particular word or phrase within a passage. There are a couple ways to approach these kinds of questions:

1. Define the word or phrase in a way that is easy to comprehend (using context clues).
2. Try out each answer choice in place of the word.

To demonstrate, here's an example from *Alice in Wonderland*:

> Alice was beginning to get very tired of sitting by her sister on the bank, and of having nothing to do: once or twice she <u>peeped</u> into the book her sister was reading, but it had no pictures or conversations in it, "and what is the use of a book," thought Alice, "without pictures or conversations?"

Q: As it is used in the selection, the word peeped means:

Using the first technique, before looking at the answers, define the word "peeped" using context clues and then find the matching answer. Then, analyze the entire passage in order to determine the meaning, not just the surrounding words.

To begin, imagine a blank where the word should be and put a synonym or definition there: "once or twice she ______ into the book her sister was reading." The context clue here is the book. It may be tempting to put "read" where the blank is, but notice the preposition word, "into." One does not read *into* a book, one simply reads a book, and since reading a book requires that it is seen with a pair of eyes, then "look" would make the most sense to put into the blank: "once or twice she looked into the book her sister was reading."

Once an easy-to-understand word or synonym has been supplanted, readers should check to make sure it makes sense with the rest of the passage. What happened after she looked into the book? She thought to herself how a book without pictures or conversations is useless. This situation in its entirety makes sense.

Now check the answer choices for a match:

a. To make a high-pitched cry
b. To smack
c. To look curiously
d. To pout

Since the word was already defined, Choice *C* is the best option.

Using the second technique, replace the figurative blank with each of the answer choices and determine which one is the most appropriate. Remember to look further into the passage to clarify that they work, because they could still make sense out of context.

a. Once or twice she made a high pitched cry into the book her sister was reading
b. Once or twice she smacked into the book her sister was reading
c. Once or twice she looked curiously into the book her sister was reading
d. Once or twice she pouted into the book her sister was reading

For Choice *A*, it does not make much sense in any context for a person to yell into a book, unless maybe something terrible has happened in the story. Given that afterward Alice thinks to herself how useless a book without pictures is, this option does not make sense within context.

For Choice *B*, smacking a book someone is reading may make sense if the rest of the passage indicates a reason for doing so. If Alice was angry or her sister had shoved it in her face, then maybe smacking the book would make sense within context. However, since whatever she does with the book causes her to think, "what is the use of a book without pictures or conversations?" then answer Choice *B* is not an appropriate answer. Answer Choice *C* fits well within context, given her subsequent thoughts on the matter. Answer Choice *D* does not make sense in context or grammatically, as people do not "pout into" things.

This is a simple example to illustrate the techniques outlined above. There may, however, be a question in which all of the definitions are correct and also make sense out of context, in which the appropriate context clues will really need to be honed in on in order to determine the correct answer. For example, here is another passage from *Alice in Wonderland*:

> . . . but when the Rabbit actually took a watch out of its waistcoat pocket, and looked at it, and then hurried on, Alice started to her feet, for it flashed across her mind that she had never before seen a rabbit with either a waistcoat-pocket or a watch to take out of it, and burning with curiosity, she ran across the field after it, and was just in time to see it pop down a large rabbit-hole under the hedge.

Q: As it is used in the passage, the word started means

a. To turn on
b. To begin
c. To move quickly
d. To be surprised

All of these words qualify as a definition of "start," but using context clues, the correct answer can be identified using one of the two techniques above. It's easy to see that one does not turn on, begin, or be surprised to one's feet. The selection also states that she "ran across the field after it," indicating that she was in a hurry. Therefore, to move quickly would make the most sense in this context.

The same strategies can be applied to vocabulary that may be completely unfamiliar. In this case, focus on the words before or after the unknown word in order to determine its definition. Take this sentence, for example:

> Sam was such a miser that he forced Andrew to pay him twelve cents for the candy, even though he had a large inheritance and he knew his friend was poor.

Unlike with assertion questions, for vocabulary questions, it may be necessary to apply some critical thinking skills that may not be explicitly stated within the passage. Think about the implications of the passage, or what the text is trying to say. With this example, it is important to realize that it is considered unusually stingy for a person to demand so little money from someone instead of just letting their friend have the candy, especially if this person is already wealthy. Hence, a miser is a greedy or stingy individual.

Questions about complex vocabulary may not be explicitly asked, but this is a useful skill to know. If there is an unfamiliar word while reading a passage and its definition goes unknown, it is possible to miss out on a critical message that could inhibit the ability to appropriately answer the questions. Practicing this technique in daily life will sharpen this ability to derive meanings from context clues with ease.

Synthesis

Synthesis in reading involves the ability to fully comprehend text passages, and then going further by making new connections to see things in a new or different way. It involves a full thought process and requires readers to change the way they think about what they read. The Accuplacer will require a test taker to integrate new information that he or she already knows, and demonstrate an ability to express new thoughts.

Synthesis goes further than summary. When summarizing, a reader collects all of the information an author presents in a text passage, and restates it in an effective manner. Synthesis requires that the test taker not only summarize reading material, but be able to express new ideas based on the author's message. It is a full culmination of all reading comprehension strategies. It will require the test taker to order, recount, summarize, and recreate information into a whole new idea.

In utilizing synthesis, a reader must be able to form mental images about what they read, recall any background information they have about the topic, ask critical questions about the material, determine the importance of points an author makes, make inferences based on the reading, and finally be able to form new ideas based on all of the above skills. Synthesis requires the reader to make connections, visualize concepts, determine their importance, ask questions, make inferences, then fully synthesize all of this information into new thought.

Making Connections in Reading

There are three helpful thinking strategies to keep in mind when attempting to synthesize text passages:

- Think about how the content of a passage relates to life experience;
- Think about how the content of a passage relates to other text and;
- Think about how the content of a passage relates to the world in general.

When reading a given passage, the test taker should actively think about how the content relates to their life experience. While the author's message may express an opinion different from what the reader believes, or express ideas with which the reader is unfamiliar, a good reader will try to relate any of the author's details to their own familiar ground. A reader should use context clues to understand unfamiliar terminology, and recognize familiar information they have encountered in prior experience. Bringing prior life experience and knowledge to the test-taking situation is helpful in making connections. The ability to relate an unfamiliar idea to something the reader already knows is critical in understanding unique and new ideas. When trying to make connections while reading, keep the following questions in mind:

- How does this feel familiar in personal experience?
- How is this similar to or different from other reading?
- How is this familiar in the real world?
- How does this relate to the world in general?

A reader should ask themself these questions during the act of reading in order to actively make connections to past and present experiences. Utilizing the ability to make connections is an important step in achieving synthesis.

Determining Importance in Reading

Being able to determine what is most important while reading is critical to synthesis. It is the difference between being able to tell what is necessary to full comprehension and that which is interesting but not necessary.

When determining the importance of an author's ideas, consider the following:

Ask how critical an author's particular idea, assertion, or concept is to the overall message.

Ask "is this an interesting fact or is this information essential to understanding the author's main idea?"

Make a simple chart. On one side, list all of the important, essential points an author makes and on the other, list all of the interesting yet non-critical ideas.

Highlight, circle, or underline any dates or data in non-fiction passages. Pay attention to headings, captions, and any graphs or diagrams.

When reading a fictional passage, delineate important information such as theme, character, setting, conflict (what the problem is), and resolution (how the problem is fixed). Most often, these are the most important aspects contained in fictional text.

If a non-fiction passage is instructional in nature, take physical note of any steps in the order of their importance as presented by the author. Look for words such as *first*, *next*, *then*, and *last*.

Determining the importance of an author's ideas is critical to synthesis in that it requires the test taker to parse out any unnecessary information and demonstrate they have the ability to make sound determination on what is important to the author, and what is merely a supporting or less critical detail.

Asking Questions While Reading

A reader must ask questions while reading. This demonstrates their ability to critically approach information and apply higher thinking skills to an author's content. Some of these questions have been addressed earlier in this section. A reader must ask what is or isn't important, what relates to their experience, and what relates to the world in general? However, it's important to ask other questions as well in order to make connections and synthesize reading material.

Consider the following partial list of possibilities:

- What type of passage is this? Is it fiction? Non-fiction? Does it include data?
- Based on the type of passage, what information should be noted in order to make connections, visualize details, and determine importance?
- What is the author's message or theme? What is it they want the reader to understand?
- Is this passage trying to convince readers of something? What is it? If so, is the argument logical, convincing, and effective? How so? If not, how not?
- What do readers already know about this topic? Are there other viewpoints that support or contradict it?
- Is the information in this passage current and up to date?
- Is the author trying to teach readers a lesson? If so, what is it? Is there a moral to this story?
- How does this passage relate to experience?
- What is not as understandable in this passage? What context clues can help with understanding?
- What conclusions can be drawn? What predictions can be made?

Again, the above should be considered only a small example of the possibilities. Any question the reader asks while reading will help achieve synthesis and full reading comprehension.

Vocabulary

Vocabulary is the words a person uses on a daily basis. Having a good vocabulary is important. It's important in writing and also when you talk to people. Many of the questions on the test may have words that you don't know. Therefore, it's important to learn ways to find out a word's meaning.

It's hard to use vocabulary correctly. Imagine being thrust into a foreign country. If you didn't know right words to use to ask for the things you need, you could run into trouble! Asking for help from people who don't share the same vocabulary is hard. Language helps us understand each other. The more vocabulary words a person knows, the easier they can ask for things they need. This section of the study guide focuses on getting to know vocabulary through basic grammar.

<u>Prefixes and Suffixes</u>

In this section, we will look at the *meaning* of various prefixes and suffixes when added to a root word. A *prefix* is a combination of letters found at the beginning of a word. A *suffix* is a combination of letters found at the end. A *root word* is the word that comes after the prefix, before the suffix, or between them both. Sometimes a root word can stand on its own without either a prefix or a suffix.

More simply put:

Prefix + Root Word = Word

Root Word + Suffix = Word

Prefix + Root Word + Suffix = Word

Root Word = Word

Knowing the definitions of common prefixes and suffixes is helpful. It's helpful when you are trying to find out the meaning of a word you don't know. Also, knowing prefixes can help you find out the number of things, the negative of something, or the time and space of an object! Understanding suffixes can help when trying to find out the meaning of an adjective, noun, or verb.

The following charts look at some of the most common prefixes, what they mean, and how they're used to find out a word's meaning:

Number and Quantity Prefixes

Prefix	**Definition**	**Example**
bi-	two	bicycle, bilateral
mono-	one, single	monopoly, monotone
poly-	many	polygamy, polygon
semi-	half, partly	semiannual, semicircle
uni-	one	unicycle, universal

Here's an example of a number prefix:

The girl rode on a *bicycle* to school.

Look at the word *bicycle*. The root word (*cycle*)comes from the Greek and means *wheel*. The prefix *bi-* means *two*. The word *bicycle* means two wheels! When you look at any bicycles, they all have two wheels. If you had a unicycle, your bike would only have one wheel, because *uni-* means *one*.

Negative Prefixes

Prefix	**Definition**	**Example**
a-	without, lack of	amoral, atypical
in-	not, opposing	inability, inverted
non-	not	nonexistent, nonstop
un-	not, reverse	unable, unspoken

Here's an example of a negative prefix:

The girl was *insensitive* to the boy who broke his leg.

Look at the word *insensitive.* In the chart above, the prefix *in-* means *not* or *opposing*. Replace the prefix with *not*. Now place *not* in front of the word *sensitive.* Now we see that the girl was "not sensitive" to the boy who broke his leg. In simpler terms, she showed that she did not care. These are easy ways to use prefixes and suffixes in order to find out what a word means.

Time and Space Prefixes

Prefix	Definition	Example
a-	in, on, of, up, to	aloof, associate
ab-	from, away, off	abstract, absent
ad-	to, towards	adept, adjacent
ante-	before, previous	antebellum, antenna
anti-	against, opposing	anticipate, antisocial
cata-	down, away, thoroughly	catacomb, catalogue
circum-	around	circumstance, circumvent
com-	with, together, very	combine, compel
contra-	against, opposing	contraband, contrast
de-	from	decrease, descend
dia- dis-	through, across, apart away, off, down, not	diagram, dialect disregard, disrespect
epi-	upon	epidemic, epiphany
ex-	out	example, exit
hypo-	under, beneath	hypoallergenic, hypothermia
inter-	among, between	intermediate, international
intra-	within	intrapersonal, intravenous
ob-	against, opposing	obtain, obscure
per-	through	permanent, persist
peri-	around	periodontal, periphery
post-	after, following	postdate, postoperative
pre-	before, previous	precede, premeditate
pro-	forward, in place of	program, propel
retro-	back, backward	retroactive, retrofit
sub-	under, beneath	submarine, substantial
super-	above, extra	superior, supersede
trans-	across, beyond, over	transform, transmit
ultra-	beyond, excessively	ultraclean, ultralight

Here's an example of a space prefix:

> The teacher's motivational speech helped *propel* her students toward greater academic achievement.

Look at the word *propel.* The prefix *pro-* means *forward. Forward* means something related to time and space. *Propel* means to drive or move in a forward direction. Therefore, knowing the prefix *pro-* helps interpret that the students are moving forward *toward greater academic achievement*.

Miscellaneous Prefixes

Prefix	Definition	Example
belli-	war, warlike	bellied, belligerent
bene-	well, good	benediction, beneficial
equi-	equal	equidistant, equinox
for-	away, off, from	forbidden, forsaken
fore-	previous	forecast, forebode
homo-	same, equal	homogeneous, homonym
hyper-	excessive, over	hyperextend, hyperactive
in-	in, into	insignificant, invasive
magn-	large	magnetic, magnificent
mal-	bad, poorly, not	maladapted, malnourished
mis-	bad, poorly, not	misplace, misguide
mor-	death	mortal, morgue
neo-	new	neoclassical, neonatal
omni-	all, everywhere	omnipotent, omnipresent
ortho-	right, straight	orthodontist, orthopedic
over-	above	overload, overstock,
pan-	all, entire	panacea, pander
para-	beside, beyond	paradigm, parameter
phil-	love, like	philanthropy, philosophic
prim-	first, early	primal, primer
re-	backward, again	reload, regress
sym-	with, together	symmetry, symbolize
vis-	to see	visual, visibility

Here's another prefix example:

The computer was *primitive*; it still had a floppy disk drive!

The word *primitive* has the prefix *prim-*. The prefix *prim-*indicates being *first* or *early*. *Primitive* means the early stages of evolution. It also could mean the historical development of something. Therefore, the sentence is saying that the computer is an older model, because it no longer has a floppy disk drive.

The charts that follow review some of the most common suffixes. They also include examples of how the suffixes are used to determine the meaning of a word. Remember, suffixes are added to the *end* of a root word:

Adjective Suffixes

Suffix	Definition	Example
-able (-ible)	capable of being	teachable, accessible
-esque	in the style of, like	humoresque, statuesque
-ful	filled with, marked by	helpful, deceitful
-ic	having, containing	manic, elastic
-ish	suggesting, like	malnourish, tarnish
-less	lacking, without	worthless, fearless
-ous	marked by, given to	generous, previous

Here's an example of an adjective suffix:

The live model looked so *statuesque* in the window display; she didn't even move!

Look at the word *statuesque*. The suffix *-esque* means *in the style of* or *like*. If something is *statuesque,* it's *like a statue*. In this sentence, the model looks like a statue.

Noun Suffixes

Suffix	Definition	Example
-acy	state, condition	literacy, legacy
-ance	act, condition, fact	distance, importance
-ard	one that does	leotard, billiard
-ation	action, state, result	legislation, condemnation
-dom	state, rank, condition	freedom, kingdom
-er (-or)	office, action	commuter, spectator
-ess	feminine	caress, princess
-hood	state, condition	childhood, livelihood
-ion	action, result, state	communion, position
-ism	act, manner, doctrine	capitalism, patriotism
-ist	worker, follower	stylist, activist
-ity (-ty)	state, quality, condition	community, dirty
-ment	result, action	empowerment, segment
-ness	quality, state	fitness, rudeness
-ship	position	censorship, leadership
-sion (-tion)	state, result	tension, transition
-th	act, state, quality	twentieth, wealth
-tude	quality, state, result	attitude, latitude

Look at the following example of a noun suffix:

The *spectator* cheered when his favorite soccer team scored a goal.

Look at the word *spectator*. The suffix *-or* means *action*. In this sentence, the *action* is to *spectate* (watch something). Therefore, a *spectator* is someone involved in watching something.

Verb Suffixes

Suffix	Definition	Example
-ate	having, showing	facilitate, integrate
-en	cause to be, become	frozen, written
-fy	make, cause to have	modify, rectify
-ize	cause to be, treat with	realize, sanitize

Here's an example of a verb suffix:

> The preschool had to *sanitize* the toys every Tuesday and Thursday.

In the word *sanitize*, the suffix *-ize* means *cause to be* or *treat with*. By adding the suffix *-ize* to the root word *sanitary*, the meaning of the word becomes active: *cause to be sanitary*.

Practice Questions

Directions for questions 1–10

Read the statement or passage and then choose the best answer to the question. Answer the question based on what is stated or implied in the statement or passage.

1. While scientists aren't entirely certain why tornadoes form, they have some clues into the process. Tornadoes are dangerous funnel clouds that occur during a large thunderstorm. When warm, humid air near the ground meets cold, dry air from above, a column of the warm air can be drawn up into the clouds. Winds at different altitudes blowing at different speeds make the column of air rotate. As the spinning column of air picks up speed, a funnel cloud is formed. This funnel cloud moves rapidly and haphazardly. Rain and hail inside the cloud cause it to touch down, creating a tornado. Tornadoes move in a rapid and unpredictable pattern, making them extremely destructive and dangerous. Scientists continue to study tornadoes to improve radar detection and warning times.

The main purpose of this passage is to:

a. Show why tornadoes are dangerous
b. Explain how a tornado forms
c. Compare thunderstorms to tornadoes
d. Explain what to do in the event of a tornado

2. There are two major kinds of cameras on the market right now for amateur photographers. Camera enthusiasts can either purchase a digital single-lens reflex camera (DSLR) camera or a compact system camera (CSC). The main difference between a DSLR and a CSC is that the DSLR has a full-sized sensor, which means it fits in a much larger body. The CSC uses a mirrorless system, which makes for a lighter, smaller camera. While both take quality pictures, the DSLR generally has better picture quality due to the larger sensor. CSCs still take very good quality pictures and are more convenient to carry than a DSLR. This makes the CSC an ideal choice for the amateur photographer looking to step up from a point-and-shoot camera.

The main difference between the DSLR and CSC is:

a. The picture quality is better in the DSLR.
b. The CSC is less expensive than the DSLR.
c. The DSLR is a better choice for amateur photographers.
d. The DSLR's larger sensor makes it a bigger camera than the CSC.

3. When selecting a career path, it's important to explore the various options available. Many students entering college may shy away from a major because they don't know much about it. For example, many students won't opt for a career as an actuary, because they aren't exactly sure what it entails. They would be missing out on a career that is very lucrative and in high demand. Actuaries work in the insurance field and assess risks and premiums. The average salary of an actuary is $100,000 per year. Another career option students may avoid, due to lack of knowledge of the field, is a hospitalist. This is a physician that specializes in the care of patients in a hospital, as opposed to those seen in private

practices. The average salary of a hospitalist is upwards of $200,000. It pays to do some digging and find out more about these lesser-known career fields.

An actuary is:

a. A doctor who works in a hospital
b. The same as a hospitalist
c. An insurance agent who works in a hospital
d. A person who assesses insurance risks and premiums

4. Many people are unsure of exactly how the digestive system works. Digestion begins in the mouth where teeth grind up food and saliva breaks it down, making it easier for the body to absorb. Next, the food moves to the esophagus, and it is pushed into the stomach. The stomach is where food is stored and broken down further by acids and digestive enzymes, preparing it for passage into the intestines. The small intestine is where the nutrients are taken from food and passed into the blood stream. Other essential organs like the liver, gall bladder, and pancreas aid the stomach in breaking down food and absorbing nutrients. Finally, food waste is passed into the large intestine where it is eliminated by the body.

The purpose of this passage is to:

a. Explain how the liver works.
b. Show why it is important to eat healthy foods
c. Explain how the digestive system works
d. Show how nutrients are absorbed by the small intestine

5. Hard water occurs when rainwater mixes with minerals from rock and soil. Hard water has a high mineral count, including calcium and magnesium. The mineral deposits from hard water can stain hard surfaces in bathrooms and kitchens as well as clog pipes. Hard water can stain dishes, ruin clothes, and reduce the life of any appliances it touches, such as hot water heaters, washing machines, and humidifiers.

One solution is to install a water softener to reduce the mineral content of water, but this can be costly. Running vinegar through pipes and appliances and using vinegar to clean hard surfaces can also help with mineral deposits.

From this passage, it can be concluded that:

a. Hard water can cause a lot of problems for homeowners.
b. Calcium is good for pipes and hard surfaces.
c. Water softeners are easy to install.
d. Vinegar is the only solution to hard water problems.

6. Osteoporosis is a medical condition that occurs when the body loses bone or makes too little bone. This can lead to brittle, fragile bones that easily break. Bones are already porous, and when osteoporosis sets in, the spaces in bones become much larger, causing them to weaken. Both men and

women can contract osteoporosis, though it is most common in women over age 50. Loss of bone can be silent and progressive, so it is important to be proactive in prevention of the disease.

The main purpose of this passage is to:

a. Discuss some of the ways people contract osteoporosis
b. Describe different treatment options for those with osteoporosis
c. Explain how to prevent osteoporosis
d. Define osteoporosis

7. Vacationers looking for a perfect experience should opt out of Disney parks and try a trip on Disney Cruise Lines. While a park offers rides, characters, and show experiences, it also includes long lines, often very hot weather, and enormous crowds. A Disney Cruise, on the other hand, is a relaxing, luxurious vacation that includes many of the same experiences as the parks, minus the crowds and lines. The cruise has top-notch food, maid service, water slides, multiple pools, Broadway-quality shows, and daily character experiences for kids. There are also many activities, such as bingo, trivia contests, and dance parties that can entertain guests of all ages. The cruise even stops at Disney's private island for a beach barbecue with characters, waterslides, and water sports. Those looking for the Disney experience without the hassle should book a Disney cruise.

The main purpose of this passage is to:

a. Explain how to book a Disney cruise
b. Show what Disney parks have to offer
c. Show why Disney parks are expensive
d. Compare Disney parks to the Disney cruise

8. Coaches of kids' sports teams are increasingly concerned about the behavior of parents at games. Parents are screaming and cursing at coaches, officials, players, and other parents. Physical fights have even broken out at games. Parents need to be reminded that coaches are volunteers, giving up their time and energy to help kids develop in their chosen sport. The goal of kids' sports teams is to learn and develop skills, but it's also to have fun. When parents are out of control at games and practices, it takes the fun out of the sport.

From this passage, it can be concluded that:

a. Coaches are modeling good behavior for kids.
b. Organized sports are not good for kids.
c. Parents' behavior at their kids' games needs to change.
d. Parents and coaches need to work together.

9. As summer approaches, drowning incidents will increase. Drowning happens very quickly and silently. Most people assume that drowning is easy to spot, but a person who is drowning doesn't make noise or wave his arms. Instead, he will have his head back and his mouth open, with just his face out of the water. A person who is truly in danger of drowning is not able to wave his arms in the air or move much at all. Recognizing these signs of drowning can prevent tragedy.

The main purpose of this passage is to:

a. Explain the dangers of swimming
b. Show how to identify the signs of drowning
c. Explain how to be a lifeguard
d. Compare the signs of drowning

10. Technology has been invading cars for the last several years, but there are some new high tech trends that are pretty amazing. It is now standard in many car models to have a rear-view camera, hands-free phone and text, and a touch screen digital display. Music can be streamed from a paired cell phone, and some displays can even be programmed with a personal photo. Sensors beep to indicate there is something in the driver's path when reversing and changing lanes. Rain-sensing windshield wipers and lights are automatic, leaving the driver with little to do but watch the road and enjoy the ride. The next wave of technology will include cars that automatically parallel park, and a self-driving car is on the horizon. These technological advances make it a good time to be a driver.

It can be concluded from this paragraph that:

Technology will continue to influence how cars are made.

b. Windshield wipers and lights are always automatic.

c. It is standard to have a rear-view camera in all cars.

d. Technology has reached its peak in cars.

This article discusses the famous poet and playwright William Shakespeare. Read it and answer questions 11-14.

People who argue that William Shakespeare is not responsible for the plays attributed to his name are known as anti-Stratfordians (from the name of Shakespeare's birthplace, Stratford-upon-Avon). The most common anti-Stratfordian claim is that William Shakespeare simply was not educated enough or from a high enough social class to have written plays overflowing with references to such a wide range of subjects like history, the classics, religion, and international culture. William Shakespeare was the son of a glove-maker, he only had a basic grade school education, and he never set foot outside of England—so how could he have produced plays of such sophistication and imagination? How could he have written in such detail about historical figures and events, or about different cultures and locations around Europe? According to anti-Stratfordians, the depth of knowledge contained in Shakespeare's plays suggests a well-traveled writer from a wealthy background with a university education, not a countryside writer like Shakespeare. But in fact, there is not much substance to such speculation, and most anti-Stratfordian arguments can be refuted with a little background about Shakespeare's time and upbringing.

First of all, those who doubt Shakespeare's authorship often point to his common birth and brief education as stumbling blocks to his writerly genius. Although it is true that Shakespeare did not come from a noble class, his father was a very *successful* glove-maker and his mother was from a very wealthy land owning family—so while Shakespeare may have had a country upbringing, he was certainly from a well-off family and would have been educated accordingly. Also, even though he did not attend university, grade school education in Shakespeare's time was actually quite rigorous and exposed students to classic drama through writers like Seneca and Ovid. It is not unreasonable to believe that Shakespeare received a very solid foundation in poetry and literature from his early schooling.

Next, anti-Stratfordians tend to question how Shakespeare could write so extensively about countries and cultures he had never visited before (for instance, several of his most famous works like *Romeo and Juliet* and *The Merchant of Venice* were set in Italy, on the opposite side of Europe!). But again, this criticism does not hold up under scrutiny. For one thing, Shakespeare was living in London, a bustling metropolis of international trade, the most populous city in England, and a political and cultural hub of Europe. In the daily crowds of people, Shakespeare would certainly have been able to meet travelers from other countries and hear firsthand accounts of life in their home country. And, in addition to the influx of information from world travelers, this was also the age of the printing press, a jump in technology that made it possible to print and circulate books much more easily than in the past. This also allowed for a freer flow of information across different countries, allowing people to read about life and ideas from throughout Europe. One needn't travel the continent in order to learn and write about its culture.

11. Which sentence contains the author's thesis?
   a. People who argue that William Shakespeare is not responsible for the plays attributed to his name are known as anti-Stratfordians.
   b. But in fact, there is not much substance to such speculation, and most anti-Stratfordian arguments can be refuted with a little background about Shakespeare's time and upbringing.
   c. It is not unreasonable to believe that Shakespeare received a very solid foundation in poetry and literature from his early schooling.
   d. Next, anti-Stratfordians tend to question how Shakespeare could write so extensively about countries and cultures he had never visited before.

12. In the first paragraph, "How could he have written in such detail about historical figures and events, or about different cultures and locations around Europe?" is an example of which of the following?
   a. Hyperbole
   b. Onomatopoeia
   c. Rhetorical question
   d. Appeal to authority

13. How does the author respond to the claim that Shakespeare was not well-educated because he did not attend university?
   a. By insisting upon Shakespeare's natural genius.
   b. By explaining grade school curriculum in Shakespeare's time.
   c. By comparing Shakespeare with other uneducated writers of his time.
   d. By pointing out that Shakespeare's wealthy parents probably paid for private tutors.

14. The word "bustling" in the third paragraph most nearly means which of the following?
   a. Busy
   b. Foreign
   c. Expensive
   d. Undeveloped

Questions 15 – 18 are based on the following two passages:

Passage A

Excerpt from *Preface to Lyrical Ballads* by William Wordsworth (1800)

From such verses the Poems in these volumes will be found distinguished at least by one mark of difference, that each of them has a worthy *purpose.* Not that I always began to write with a distinct purpose formerly conceived; but habits of meditation have, I trust, so prompted and regulated my feelings, that my descriptions of such objects as strongly excite those feelings, will be found to carry along with them a *purpose.* If this opinion be erroneous, I can have little right to the name of a Poet. For all good poetry is the spontaneous overflow of powerful feelings: and though this be true, Poems to which any value can be attached were never produced on any variety of subjects but by a man who, being possessed of more than usual organic sensibility, had also thought long and deeply. For our continued influxes of feeling are modified and directed by our thoughts, which are indeed the representatives of all our past feelings; and, as by contemplating the relation of these general representatives to each other, we discover what is really important to men, so, by the repetition and continuance of this act, our feelings will be connected with important subjects, till at length, if we be originally possessed of much sensibility, such habits of mind will be produced, that, by obeying blindly and mechanically the impulses of those habits, we shall describe objects, and utter sentiments, of such a nature, and in such connexion with each other, that the understanding of the Reader must necessarily be in some degree enlightened, and his affections strengthened and purified.

Passage B

Excerpt from Tradition and the Individual Talent by T.S. Eliot (1921)

If you compare several representative passages of the greatest poetry you see how great is the variety of types of combination, and also how completely any semi-ethical criterion of "sublimity" misses the mark. For it is not the "greatness," the intensity, of the emotions, the components, but the intensity of the artistic process, the pressure, so to speak, under which the fusion takes place, that counts. The episode of Paolo and Francesca employs a definite emotion, but the intensity of the poetry is something quite different from whatever intensity in the supposed experience it may give the impression of. It is no more intense, furthermore, than Canto XXVI, the voyage of Ulysses, which has not the direct dependence upon an emotion. Great variety is possible in the process of transmution of emotion: the murder of Agamemnon, or the agony of Othello, gives an artistic effect apparently closer to a possible original than the scenes from Dante. In the *Agamemnon,* the artistic emotion approximates to the emotion of an actual spectator; in *Othello* to the emotion of the protagonist himself. But the difference between art and the event is always absolute; the combination which is the murder of Agamemnon is probably as complex as that which is the voyage of Ulysses. In either case there has been a fusion of elements. The ode of Keats contains a number of feelings which have nothing particular to do with the nightingale, but which the nightingale, partly, perhaps, because of its attractive name, and partly because of its reputation, served to bring together.

15. Which one of the following most accurately characterizes the relationship between the two passages?

  a. Passage A offers an explanation of the purpose of poetry, while passage B offers an explanation of the results of poetry.
  b. Passage A is concerned with the context of poetry involving nature, while passage B is concerned with the context of poetry involving urban life.
  c. Passage A focuses on lyric poetry, while passage B is concerned with epic poetry.
  d. Passage A argues that the source of great poetry comes from emotions within, while passage B argues that great poetry is based off the skill and expertise of the poet.

16. What does the author of passage B mean by the last sentence?

a. The author is explaining that the feelings portrayed in Keats' ode are brought forth and signified by the symbolism of the nightingale used within the language of the poem.

b. The author means that Keats' poetry is more valuable than epic verse because the feelings expressed in his poetry are backed by literary talent.

c. The author means that the figure of the nightingale serves a myriad of purposes; here, for a symbolic use of a range of emotions such as grief, fear, and sorrow.

d. The author is trying to argue that the reputation of the poet serves to bring about the feelings of the reader; or, that the ethos of the writing is closely related to the pathos in the audience.

17. The author of passage A thinks which of the following about thoughts and feelings as they relate to poetry?

a. That the thoughts of the poet are the primary source of inspiration, and that feeling is a secondary motivation for the poet. Once the poet gets their thoughts onto paper, the feelings of the poet will come after.

b. That thoughts and feelings are one and the same thing; that they happen simultaneously, and that this merging creates the perfect condition to write a poem.

c. That feelings from the past will accumulate into representations of thought. The poet is then responsible for putting these direct thoughts onto paper, creating a poem. Therefore, the original source of poetry is from the past feelings of the poet.

d. That thoughts and feelings are overrated; namely, that critics of the past have put too much emphasis on thoughts and feelings as they relate to poetry.

18. The authors of the passages differ in their explanations of great poetry in that the author of passage B

a. argues that the intensity of the emotion felt while writing the poem counts for more than the effort put into a poem.

b. argues that the effort put into a poem counts for more than the intensity of the emotion felt while writing the poem.

c. argues that the purpose of poetry is for the reader to feel an emotional connection with the author.

d. argues that good poetry is produced by poets who think long and deeply about their subjects before they write about it.

Below there is a blank in each question. Choose the word or phrase in the answer choice that best fits the meaning of the sentence as a whole.

19. Before she put a down payment on the house, the would-be buyer had to make sure the house was properly __________ first.

a. Vacated

b. Dilapidated

c. Inspected

d. Insulated

20. The time had come when Deirdre knew she had to __________ her position at her company in order to go back to school and earn a degree.

a. Relinquish
b. Rearrange
c. Reciprocate
d. Receive

Answer Explanations

1. B: The main point of this passage is to show how a tornado forms. Choice *A* is off base because while the passage does mention that tornadoes are dangerous, it is not the main focus of the passage. While thunderstorms are mentioned, they are not compared to tornadoes, so Choice *C* is incorrect. Choice *D* is incorrect because the passage does not discuss what to do in the event of a tornado.

2. D: The passage directly states that the larger sensor is the main difference between the two cameras. Choices *A* and *B* may be true, but these answers do not identify the major difference between the two cameras. Choice *C* states the opposite of what the paragraph suggests is the best option for amateur photographers, so it is incorrect.

3. D: An actuary assesses risks and sets insurance premiums. While an actuary does work in insurance, the passage does not suggest that actuaries have any affiliation with hospitalists or working in a hospital, so all other choices are incorrect.

4. C: The purpose of this passage is to explain how the digestive system works. Choice *A* focuses only on the liver, which is a small part of the process and not the focus of the paragraph. Choice *B* is off-track because the passage does not mention healthy foods. Choice *D* only focuses on one part of the digestive system.

5. A: The passage focuses mainly on the problems of hard water. Choice *B* is incorrect because calcium is not good for pipes and hard surfaces. The passage does not say anything about whether water softeners are easy to install, so *C* is incorrect. *D* is also incorrect because the passage does offer other solutions besides vinegar.

6. D: The main point of this passage is to define osteoporosis. Choice *A* is incorrect because the passage does not list ways that people contract osteoporosis. Choice *B* is incorrect because the passage does not mention any treatment options. While the passage does briefly mention prevention, it does not explain how, so Choice *C* is incorrect.

7. D: The passage compares Disney cruises with Disney parks. It does not discuss how to book a cruise, so Choice *A* is incorrect. Choice *B* is incorrect because though the passage does mention some of the park attractions, it is not the main point. The passage does not mention the cost of either option, so Choice *C* is incorrect.

8. C: The main point of this paragraph is that parents need to change their poor behavior at their kids' sporting events. Choice *A* is incorrect because the coaches' behavior is not mentioned in the paragraph. *B* suggests that sports are bad for kids, when the paragraph is about parents' behavior, so it is incorrect. While Choice *D* may be true, it offers a specific solution to the problem, which the paragraph does not discuss.

9. B: The point of this passage is to show what drowning looks like. Choice *A* is incorrect because while drowning is a danger of swimming, the passage doesn't include any other dangers. The passage is not intended for lifeguards specifically, but for a general audience, so Choice *C* is incorrect. There are a few signs of drowning, but the passage does not compare them; thus, Choice *D* is incorrect.

10. A: The passage discusses recent technological advances in cars and suggests that this trend will continue in the future with self-driving cars. Choice *B* and *C* are not true, so these are both incorrect. Choice *D* is also incorrect because the passage suggests continuing growth in technology, not a peak.

11. B: But in fact, there is not much substance to such speculation, and most anti-Stratfordian arguments can be refuted with a little background about Shakespeare's time and upbringing. The thesis is a statement that contains the author's topic and main idea. The main purpose of this article is to use historical evidence to provide counterarguments to anti-Stratfordians. Choice *A* is simply a definition; Choice *C* is a supporting detail, not a main idea; and Choice *D* represents an idea of anti-Stratfordians, not the author's opinion.

12. C: Rhetorical question. This requires readers to be familiar with different types of rhetorical devices. A rhetorical question is a question that is asked not to obtain an answer but to encourage readers to more deeply consider an issue.

13. B: By explaining grade school curriculum in Shakespeare's time. This question asks readers to refer to the organizational structure of the article and demonstrate understanding of how the author provides details to support their argument. This particular detail can be found in the second paragraph: "even though he did not attend university, grade school education in Shakespeare's time was actually quite rigorous."

14. A: Busy. This is a vocabulary question that can be answered using context clues. Other sentences in the paragraph describe London as "the most populous city in England" filled with "crowds of people," giving an image of a busy city full of people. Choice *B* is incorrect because London was in Shakespeare's home country, not a foreign one. Choice *C* is not mentioned in the passage. Choice *D* is not a good answer choice because the passage describes how London was a popular and important city, probably not an underdeveloped one.

15. D: Passage A argues that the source of great poetry comes from emotions within, while passage B argues that great poetry is based off the skill and expertise of the poet. Choice *A* is incorrect; both passages attempt to explain how great poetry is created, not its aim or its results. The "purpose" passage A talks about are the author's individual poems, but the main idea of the passage is contained in the middle, starting with "For all good poetry." Choice *B* is incorrect; neither passages make any mention of nature or urban life. Choice *C* is incorrect; passage B does use epic poetry for most of its examples, but it is not solely concerned with epic poetry. It recalls Keats' "Ode to a Nightingale" at the very end. This is not the best answer choice.

16. A: The author is explaining that the feelings portrayed in Keats' ode are brought forth and signified by the symbolism of the nightingale used within the language of the poem. Eliot is relating it back to the original point of the passage: that great poetry doesn't simply come from powerful emotion, but that it is that emotion coupled with the literary devices of the poet that makes great poetry. Some of the other choices have similar wording to the last sentence, but they are not the best answer choice.

17. C: That feelings from the past will accumulate into representations of thought. The poet is then responsible for putting these direct thoughts onto paper, creating a poem. Therefore, the original source of poetry is from the past feelings of the poet. This is explained by the author beginning with the sentence "For our continued influxes of feeling . . . " The author is very clear about feelings from the past accumulating into representations of thought, so all the other answer choices are incorrect.

18. B: The author of passage B argues that the effort put into a poem counts for more than the intensity of the emotion felt while writing the poem. Choice *A* is the opposite of what passage B argues. Choices *C* and *D* are more closely related to the ideas of passage A.

19. C: The best word here is inspected, which means *approved* or *investigated*. Choice *A*, vacated, means to leave empty. While this is a possible choice, it is not the best choice. Choice *B*, dilapidated, means destroyed. Someone buying a house does not want the house to be left destroyed, so this is incorrect. Choice *D,* insulated, means that the house would be properly enclosed against the loss of heat or the intrusion of sound. Although this is a possible answer, this would be included in an inspection. Therefore, Choice *D* is incorrect.

20. A: Relinquish. Relinquish most closely means to give up or let go. Deirdre knew she had to give up her position in order to go back to school. Choice *B*, rearrange, means to shift or change. Choice *C*, reciprocate, means to exchange or swap. Choice *D*, receive, means to accept.

Writing

Expression of Ideas

Development

Brainstorming

One of the most important steps in writing an essay is prewriting. Before drafting an essay, it's helpful to think about the topic for a moment or two, in order to gain a more solid understanding of what the task is. Then, spending about five minutes jotting down the immediate ideas that could work for the essay is recommended. It is a way to get some words on the page and offer a reference for ideas when drafting. Scratch paper is provided for writers to use any prewriting techniques such as webbing, free writing, or listing. The goal is to get ideas out of the mind and onto the page.

Considering Opposing Viewpoints

In the planning stage, it's important to consider all aspects of the topic, including different viewpoints on the subject. There are more than two ways to look at a topic, and a strong argument considers those opposing viewpoints. Considering opposing viewpoints can help writers present a fair, balanced, and informed essay that shows consideration for all readers. This approach can also strengthen an argument by recognizing and potentially refuting the opposing viewpoint(s).

Drawing from personal experience may help to support ideas. For example, if the goal for writing is a personal narrative, then the story should be from the writer's own life. Many writers find it helpful to draw from personal experience, even in an essay that is not strictly narrative. Personal anecdotes or short stories can help to illustrate a point in other types of essays as well.

Moving from Brainstorming to Planning

Once the ideas are on the page, it's time to turn them into a solid plan for the essay. The best ideas from the brainstorming results can then be developed into a more formal outline. An outline typically has one main point (the thesis) and at least three sub-points that support the main point. Here's an example:

Main Idea

- Point #1
- Point #2
- Point #3

Of course, there will be details under each point, but this approach is the best for dealing with timed writing.

Staying on Track

Basing the essay on the outline aids in both organization and coherence. The goal is to ensure that there is enough time to develop each sub-point in the essay, roughly spending an equal amount of time on each idea. Keeping an eye on the time will help. If there are fifteen minutes left to draft the essay, then it makes sense to spend about 5 minutes on each of the ideas. Staying on task is critical to success, and timing out the parts of the essay can help writers avoid feeling overwhelmed.

Parts of the Essay

The *introduction* has to do a few important things:

- Establish the *topic* of the essay in original wording (i.e., not just repeating the prompt)
- Clarify the significance/importance of the topic or purpose for writing (not too many details, a brief overview)
- Offer a *thesis statement* that identifies the writer's own viewpoint on the topic (typically one-two brief sentences as a clear, concise explanation of the main point on the topic)

Body paragraphs reflect the ideas developed in the outline. Three-four points is probably sufficient for a short essay, and they should include the following:

- A *topic sentence* that identifies the sub-point (e.g., a reason why, a way how, a cause or effect)
- A detailed *explanation* of the point, explaining why the writer thinks this point is valid
- Illustrative *examples*, such as personal examples or real world examples, that support and validate the point (i.e., "prove" the point)
- A *concluding sentence* that connects the examples, reasoning, and analysis to the point being made

The *conclusion*, or final paragraph, should be brief and should reiterate the focus, clarifying why the discussion is significant or important. It is important to avoid adding specific details or new ideas to this paragraph. The purpose of the conclusion is to sum up what has been said to bring the discussion to a close.

Don't Panic!

Writing an essay can be overwhelming, and performance panic is a natural response. The outline serves as a basis for the writing and help writers keep focused. Getting stuck can also happen, and it's helpful to remember that brainstorming can be done at any time during the writing process. Following the steps of the writing process is the best defense against writer's block.

Timed essays can be particularly stressful, but assessors are trained to recognize the necessary planning and thinking for these timed efforts. Using the plan above and sticking to it helps with time management. Timing each part of the process helps writers stay on track. Sometimes writers try to cover too much in their essays. If time seems to be running out, this is an opportunity to determine whether all of the ideas in the outline are necessary. Three body paragraphs is sufficient, and more than that is probably too much to cover in a short essay.

More isn't always *better* in writing. A strong essay will be clear and concise. It will avoid unnecessary or repetitive details. It is better to have a concise, five-paragraph essay that makes a clear point, than a ten-paragraph essay that doesn't. The goal is to write one-two pages of quality writing. Paragraphs should also reflect balance; if the introduction goes to the bottom of the first page, the writing may be going off-track or be repetitive. It's best to fall into the one-two page range, but a complete, well-developed essay is the ultimate goal.

The Final Steps

Leaving a few minutes at the end to revise and proofread offers an opportunity for writers to polish things up. Putting one's self in the reader's shoes and focusing on what the essay actually says helps writers identify problems—it's a movement from the mindset of writer to the mindset of editor. The goal is to have a clean, clear copy of the essay. The following areas should be considered when proofreading:

- Sentence fragments
- Awkward sentence structure
- Run-on sentences
- Incorrect word choice
- Grammatical agreement errors
- Spelling errors
- Punctuation errors
- Capitalization errors

The Short Overview

The essay may seem challenging, but following these steps can help writers focus:

- Take one-two minutes to think about the topic.
- Generate some ideas through brainstorming (three-four minutes).
- Organize ideas into a brief outline, selecting just three-four main points to cover in the essay (eventually the body paragraphs).
- Develop essay in parts:
- Introduction paragraph, with intro to topic and main points
- Viewpoint on the subject at the end of the introduction
- Body paragraphs, based on outline
- Each paragraph: makes a main point, explains the viewpoint, uses examples to support the point
- Brief conclusion highlighting the main points and closing
- Read over the essay (last five minutes).
- Look for any obvious errors, making sure that the writing makes sense.

Organization

Good writing is not merely a random collection of sentences. No matter how well written, sentences must relate and coordinate appropriately with one another. If not, the writing seems random, haphazard, and disorganized. Therefore, good writing must be organized, where each sentence fits a larger context and relates to the sentences around it.

Transition Words

The writer should act as a guide, showing the reader how all the sentences fit together. Consider the seat belt example again:

> Seat belts save more lives than any other automobile safety feature. Many studies show that airbags save lives as well. Not all cars have airbags. Many older cars don't. Air bags aren't entirely reliable. Studies show that in 15% of accidents, airbags don't deploy as designed. Seat belt malfunctions are extremely rare.

There's nothing wrong with any of these sentences individually, but together they're disjointed and difficult to follow. The best way for the writer to communicate information is through the use of transition words. Here are examples of transition words and phrases that tie sentences together, enabling a more natural flow:

- To show causality: as a result, therefore, and consequently
- To compare and contrast: *however*, *but*, and *on the other hand*
- To introduce examples: *for instance*, *namely*, and *including*
- To show order of importance: *foremost*, *primarily*, *secondly*, and *lastly*

NOTE: This is not a complete list of transitions. There are many more that can be used; however, most fit into these or similar categories. The important point is that the words should clearly show the relationship between sentences, supporting information, and the main idea.

Here is an update to the previous example using transition words. These changes make it easier to read and bring clarity to the writer's points:

> Seat belts save more lives than any other automobile safety feature. Many studies show that airbags save lives as well; however, not all cars have airbags. For instance, some older cars don't. Furthermore, air bags aren't entirely reliable. For example, studies show that in 15% of accidents, airbags don't deploy as designed, but, on the other hand, seat belt malfunctions are extremely rare.

Also be prepared to analyze whether the writer is using the best transition word or phrase for the situation. Take this sentence for example: "As a result, seat belt malfunctions are extremely rare." This sentence doesn't make sense in the context above because the writer is trying to show the contrast between seat belts and airbags, not the causality.

<u>Logical Sequence</u>

Even if the writer includes plenty of information to support their point, the writing is only coherent when the information is in a logical order. First, the writer should introduce the main idea, whether for a paragraph, a section, or the entire piece. Then they should present evidence to support the main idea by using transitional language. This shows the reader how the information relates to the main idea and to the sentences around it. The writer should then take time to interpret the information, making sure necessary connections are obvious to the reader. Finally, the writer can summarize the information in a closing section.

Though most writing follows this pattern, it isn't a set rule. Sometimes writers change the order for effect. For example, the writer can begin with a surprising piece of supporting information to grab the reader's attention, and then transition to the main idea. Thus, if a passage doesn't follow the logical order, don't immediately assume it's wrong. However, most writing usually settles into a logical sequence after a nontraditional beginning.

Introductions and Conclusions

Examining the writer's strategies for introductions and conclusions puts the reader in the right mindset to interpret the rest of the text. Look for methods the writer might use for introductions such as:

- Stating the main point immediately, followed by outlining how the rest of the piece supports this claim.

- Establishing important, smaller pieces of the main idea first, and then grouping these points into a case for the main idea.

- Opening with a quotation, anecdote, question, seeming paradox, or other piece of interesting information, and then using it to lead to the main point.

Whatever method the writer chooses, the introduction should make their intention clear, establish their voice as a credible one, and encourage a person to continue reading.

Conclusions tend to follow a similar pattern. In them, the writer restates their main idea a final time, often after summarizing the smaller pieces of that idea. If the introduction uses a quote or anecdote to grab the reader's attention, the conclusion often makes reference to it again. Whatever way the writer chooses to arrange the conclusion, the final restatement of the main idea should be clear and simple for the reader to interpret. Finally, conclusions shouldn't introduce any new information.

Effective Language Use

Precision

People often think of precision in terms of math, but precise word choice is another key to successful writing. Since language itself is imprecise, it's important for the writer to find the exact word or words to convey the full, intended meaning of a given situation. For example:

> The number of deaths has gone down since seat belt laws started.

There are several problems with this sentence. First, the word *deaths* is too general. From the context, it's assumed that the writer is referring only to deaths caused by car accidents. However, without clarification, the sentence lacks impact and is probably untrue. The phrase "gone down" might be accurate, but a more precise word could provide more information and greater accuracy. Did the numbers show a slow and steady decrease of highway fatalities or a sudden drop? If the latter is true, the writer is missing a chance to make their point more dramatically. Instead of "gone down" they could substitute *plummeted*, *fallen drastically*, or *rapidly diminished* to bring the information to life. Also, the phrase "seat belt laws" is unclear. Does it refer to laws requiring cars to include seat belts or to laws requiring drivers and passengers to use them? Finally, *started* is not a strong verb. Words like *enacted* or *adopted* are more direct and make the content more real. When put together, these changes create a far more powerful sentence:

> The number of highway fatalities has plummeted since laws requiring seat belt usage were enacted.

However, it's important to note that precise word choice can sometimes be taken too far. If the writer of the sentence above takes precision to an extreme, it might result in the following:

The incidence of high-speed, automobile accident related fatalities has decreased 75% and continued to remain at historical lows since the initial set of federal legislations requiring seat belt use were enacted in 1992.

This sentence is extremely precise, but it takes so long to achieve that precision that it suffers from a lack of clarity. Precise writing is about finding the right balance between information and flow. This is also an issue of conciseness (discussed in the next section).

The last thing to consider with precision is a word choice that's not only unclear or uninteresting, but also confusing or misleading. For example:

The number of highway fatalities has become hugely lower since laws requiring seat belt use were enacted.

In this case, the reader might be confused by the word *hugely*. Huge means large, but here the writer uses *hugely* to describe something small. Though most readers can decipher this, doing so disconnects them from the flow of the writing and makes the writer's point less effective.

Conciseness

"Less is more" is a good rule to follow when writing a sentence. Unfortunately, writers often include extra words and phrases that seem necessary at the time, but add nothing to the main idea. This confuses the reader and creates unnecessary repetition. Writing that lacks conciseness is usually guilty of excessive wordiness and redundant phrases. Here's an example containing both of these issues:

> When legislators decided to begin creating legislation making it mandatory for automobile drivers and passengers to make use of seat belts while in cars, a large number of them made those laws for reasons that were political reasons.

There are several empty or "fluff" words here that take up too much space. These can be eliminated while still maintaining the writer's meaning. For example:

- "Decided to begin" could be shortened to "began"
- "Making it mandatory for" could be shortened to "requiring"
- "Make use of" could be shortened to "use"
- "A large number" could be shortened to "many"

In addition, there are several examples of redundancy that can be eliminated:

- "Legislators decided to begin creating legislation" and "made those laws"
- "Automobile drivers and passengers" and "while in cars"
- "Reasons that were political reasons"

These changes are incorporated as follows:

> When legislators began requiring drivers and passengers to use seat belts, many of them did so for political reasons.

There are many general examples of redundant phrases, such as "add an additional," "complete and total," "time schedule," and "transportation vehicle." If asked to identify a redundant phrase on the test, look for words that are close together with the same (or similar) meanings.

Standard English Conventions

Sentence Structure

<u>Sentence Types</u>
There are four ways in which we can structure sentences: simple, compound, complex, and compound-complex. Sentences can be composed of just one clause or many clauses joined together.

When a sentence is composed of just one clause (an independent clause), we call it a simple sentence. Simple sentences do not necessarily have to be short sentences. They just require one independent clause with a subject and a predicate. For example:

> Thomas marched over to Andrew's house.
>
> Jonah and Mary constructed a simplified version of the Eiffel Tower with Legos.

When a sentence has two or more independent clauses we call it a compound sentence. The clauses are connected by a comma and a coordinating conjunction—*and, but, or, nor, for*—or by a semicolon. Compound sentences do not have dependent clauses. For example:

> We went to the fireworks stand, and we bought enough fireworks to last all night.
>
> The children sat on the grass, and then we lit the fireworks one at a time.

When a sentence has just one independent clause and includes one or more dependent clauses, we call it a complex sentence:

> Because she slept well and drank coffee, Sarah was quite productive at work.
>
> Although Will had coffee, he made mistakes while using the photocopier.

When a sentence has two or more independent clauses and at least one dependent clause, we call it a compound-complex sentence:

> It may come as a surprise, but I found the tickets, and you can go to the show.
>
> Jade is the girl who dove from the high-dive, and she stunned the audience silent.

<u>Sentence Fragments</u>
Remember that a complete sentence must have both a subject and a verb. Complete sentences consist of at least one independent clause. Incomplete sentences are called sentence fragments. A sentence fragment is a common error in writing. Sentence fragments can be independent clauses that start with subordinating words, such as *but, as, so that,* or *because,* or they could simply be missing a subject or verb.

You can correct a fragment error by adding the fragment to a nearby sentence or by adding or removing words to make it an independent clause. For example:

> Dogs are my favorite animals. Because cats are too independent. (Incorrect; the word because creates a sentence fragment)
>
> Dogs are my favorite animals because cats are too independent. (Correct; the fragment becomes a dependent clause.)
>
> Dogs are my favorite animals. Cats are too independent. (Correct; the fragment becomes a simple sentence.)

<u>Run-on Sentences</u>

Another common mistake in writing is the run-on sentence. A run-on is created when two or more independent clauses are joined without the use of a conjunction, a semicolon, a colon, or a dash. We don't want to use commas where periods belong. Here is an example of a run-on sentence:

> Making wedding cakes can take many hours I am very impatient, I want to see them completed right away.

There are a variety of ways to correct a run-on sentence. The method you choose will depend on the context of the sentence and how it fits with neighboring sentences:

> Making wedding cakes can take many hours. I am very impatient. I want to see them completed right away. (Use periods to create more than one sentence.)
>
> Making wedding cakes can take many hours; I am very impatient—I want to see them completed right away. (Correct the sentence using a semicolon, colon, or dash.)
>
> Making wedding cakes can take many hours and I am very impatient, so I want to see them completed right away. (Correct the sentence using coordinating conjunctions.)
>
> I am very impatient because I would rather see completed wedding cakes right away than wait for it to take many hours. (Correct the sentence by revising.)

<u>Dangling and Misplaced Modifiers</u>

A modifier is a word or phrase meant to describe or clarify another word in the sentence. When a sentence has a modifier but is missing the word it describes or clarifies, it's an error called a dangling modifier. We can fix the sentence by revising to include the word that is being modified. Consider the following examples with the modifier italicized:

> *Having walked five miles*, this bench will be the place to rest. (Incorrect; this version of the sentence implies that the bench walked the miles, not the person.)
>
> *Having walked five miles,* Matt will rest on this bench. (Correct; in this version, *having walked five miles* correctly modifies *Matt*, who did the walking.)
>
> *Since midnight,* my dreams have been pleasant and comforting. (Incorrect; in this version, the adverb clause *since midnight* cannot modify the noun *dreams*.)
>
> *Since midnight,* I have had pleasant and comforting dreams. (Correct; in this version, *since midnight* modifies the verb *have had*, telling us when the dreams occurred.)

Sometimes the modifier is not located close enough to the word it modifies for the sentence to be clearly understood. In this case, we call the error a misplaced modifier. Here is an example with the modifier italicized and the modified word in underlined.

> We gave the hot <u>cocoa</u> to the children *that was filled with marshmallows.* (Incorrect; this sentence implies that the children are what are filled with marshmallows.)

> We gave the hot <u>*cocoa*</u> *that was filled with marshmallows* to the children. (Correct; here, the cocoa is filled with marshmallows. The modifier is near the word it modifies.)

<u>Parallelism and Subordination</u>

Parallelism

To be grammatically correct we must use articles, prepositions, infinitives, and introductory words for dependent clauses consistently throughout a sentence. This is called parallelism. We use parallelism when we are matching parts of speech, phrases, or clauses with another part of the sentence. Being inconsistent creates confusion. Consider the following example.

> *Incorrect:* Be ready for running and to ride a bike during the triathlon.

> *Correct:* Be ready to run and to ride a bike during the triathlon.

> *Correct:* Be ready for running and for riding a bike during the triathlon.

In the incorrect example, the gerund *running* does not match with the infinitive *to ride*. Either both should be infinitives or both should be gerunds.

Subordination

Sometimes we have unequal pieces of information in a sentence where one piece is more important than the other. We need to show that one piece of information is subordinate to the other. We can make the more important piece an independent clause and connect the other piece by making it a dependent clause. Consider this example:

> *Central thought:* Kittens can always find their mother.

> *Subordinate:* Kittens are blind at birth.

> *Complex Sentence:* Despite being blind at birth, kittens can always find their mother.

The sentence "Kittens are blind at birth" is made subordinate to the sentence "Kittens can always find their mother" by placing the word "Despite" at the beginning and removing the subject, thus turning an independent clause ("kittens are blind at birth") into a subordinate phrase ("Despite being blind at birth").

Usage

<u>Nouns</u>

A noun is a person, place, thing ,or idea. All nouns fit into one of two types, common or proper.

A *common noun* is a word that identifies any of a class of people, places, or things. Examples include numbers, objects, animals, feelings, concepts, qualities, and actions. *A, an,* or *the* usually precedes the common noun. These parts of speech are called *articles*. Here are some examples of sentences using nouns preceded by articles.

> *A* building is under construction.
> *The* girl would like to move to *the* city.

A *proper noun* (also called a *proper name*) is used for the specific name of an individual person, place, or organization. The first letter in a proper noun is capitalized. "My name is *Mary*." "I work for *Walmart*."

Nouns sometimes serve as adjectives (which themselves describe nouns), such as "hockey player" and "state government."

An abstract noun is an idea, state, or quality. It is something that can't be touched, such as happiness, courage, evil, or humor.

A concrete noun is something that can be experienced through the senses (touch, taste, hear, smell, see). Examples of concrete nouns are birds, skateboard, pie, and car.

A collective noun refers to a collection of people, places, or things that act as one. Examples of collective nouns are as follows: team, class, jury, family, audience, and flock.

<u>Pronouns</u>

A word used in place of a noun is known as a *pronoun*. Pronouns are words like *I, mine, hers,* and *us*.

Pronouns can be split into different classifications (seen below) which make them easier to learn; however, it's not important to memorize the classifications.

- Personal pronouns: refer to people
- First person: we, I, our, mine
- Second person: you, yours
- Third person: he, them
- Possessive pronouns: demonstrate ownership (mine, my, his, yours)
- Interrogative pronouns: ask questions (what, which, who, whom, whose)
- Relative pronouns: include the five interrogative pronouns and others that are relative (whoever, whomever, that, when, where)
- Demonstrative pronouns: replace something specific (this, that, those, these)
- Reciprocal pronouns: indicate something was done or given in return (each other, one another)
- Indefinite pronouns: have a nonspecific status (anybody, whoever, someone, everybody, somebody)

Indefinite pronouns such as *anybody, whoever, someone, everybody*, and *somebody* command a singular verb form, but others such as *all, none,* and *some* could require a singular or plural verb form.

Antecedents

An *antecedent* is the noun to which a pronoun refers; it needs to be written or spoken before the pronoun is used. For many pronouns, antecedents are imperative for clarity. In particular, many of the personal, possessive, and demonstrative pronouns need antecedents. Otherwise, it would be unclear who or what someone is referring to when they use a pronoun like *he* or *this*.

Pronoun reference means that the pronoun should refer clearly to one, clear, unmistakable noun (the antecedent).

Pronoun-antecedent agreement refers to the need for the antecedent and the corresponding pronoun to agree in gender, person, and number. Here are some examples:

> The *kidneys* (plural antecedent) are part of the urinary system. *They* (plural pronoun) serve several roles."

> The kidneys are part of the *urinary system* (singular antecedent). *It* (singular pronoun) is also known as the renal system.

Pronoun Cases

The subjective pronouns —*I, you, he/she/it, we, they,* and *who*—are the subjects of the sentence.

> Example: *They* have a new house.

The objective pronouns—*me, you* (*singular*), *him/her, us, them,* and *whom*—are used when something is being done for or given to someone; they are objects of the action.

> Example: The teacher has an apple for *us*.

The possessive pronouns—*mine, my, your, yours, his, hers, its, their, theirs, our,* and *ours*—are used to denote that something (or someone) belongs to someone (or something).

> Example: It's *their* chocolate cake.
> Even Better Example: It's *my* chocolate cake!

One of the greatest challenges and worst abuses of pronouns concerns *who* and *whom*. Just knowing the following rule can eliminate confusion. *Who* is a subjective-case pronoun used only as a subject or subject complement. *Whom* is only objective-case and, therefore, the object of the verb or preposition.

> *Who* is going to the concert?

> You are going to the concert with *whom*?

Hint: When using *who* or *whom*, think of whether someone would say *he* or *him*. If the answer is *he*, use *who*. If the answer is *him*, use *whom*. This trick is easy to remember because *he* and *who* both end in vowels, and *him* and *whom* both end in the letter *M*.

Verbs

The *verb* is the part of speech that describes an action, state of being, or occurrence.

A *verb* forms the main part of a predicate of a sentence. This means that the verb explains what the noun (which will be discussed shortly) is doing. A simple example is *time flies*. The verb *flies* explains what the action of the noun, *time*, is doing. This example is a *main* verb.

Helping (*auxiliary*) verbs are words like *have, do, be, can, may, should, must,* and *will.* "I *should* go to the store." Helping verbs assist main verbs in expressing tense, ability, possibility, permission, or obligation.

Particles are minor function words like *not, in, out, up,* or *down* that become part of the verb itself. "I might *not*."

Participles are words formed from verbs that are often used to modify a noun, noun phrase, verb, or verb phrase.

The *running* teenager collided with the cyclist.

Participles can also create compound verb forms.

He is *speaking*.

Verbs have five basic forms: the *base* form, the *-s* form, the *-ing* form, the *past* form, and the *past participle* form.

The *past* forms are either *regular* (*love/loved; hate/hated*) or *irregular* because they don't end by adding the common past tense suffix "-ed" (*go/went; fall/fell; set/set*).

<u>Verb Forms</u>

Shifting verb forms entails *conjugation*, which is used to indicate *tense, voice,* or *mood*.

Verb tense is used to show when the action in the sentence took place. There are several different verb tenses, and it is important to know how and when to use them. Some verb tenses can be achieved by changing the form of the verb, while others require the use of helping verbs (e.g., *is, was,* or *has*).

- Present tense shows the action is happening currently or is ongoing:

  I walk to work every morning.

  She is stressed about the deadline.

- Past tense shows that the action happened in the past or that the state of being is in the past:

  I walked to work yesterday morning.

  She was stressed about the deadline.

- Future tense shows that the action will happen in the future or is a future state of being:

  I will walk to work tomorrow morning.

  She will be stressed about the deadline.

- Present perfect tense shows action that began in the past, but continues into the present:

  I have walked to work all week.

  She has been stressed about the deadline.

- Past perfect tense shows an action was finished before another took place:

  I had walked all week until I sprained my ankle.

  She had been stressed about the deadline until we talked about it.

- Future perfect tense shows an action that will be completed at some point in the future:

  By the time the bus arrives, I will have walked to work already.

<u>Voice</u>

Verbs can be in the active or passive voice. When the subject completes the action, the verb is in *active voice*. When the subject receives the action of the sentence, the verb is in *passive voice*.

Active: Jamie ate the ice cream.

Passive: The ice cream was eaten by Jamie.

In active voice, the subject (*Jamie*) is the "do-er" of the action (*ate*). In passive voice, the subject *ice cream* receives the action of being eaten.

While passive voice can add variety to writing, active voice is the generally preferred sentence structure.

<u>Mood</u>

Mood is used to show the speaker's feelings about the subject matter. In English, there is *indicative mood, imperative mood,* and *subjective mood.*

Indicative mood is used to state facts, ask questions, or state opinions:

Bob will make the trip next week.

When can Bob make the trip?

Imperative mood is used to state a command or make a request:

Wait in the lobby.

Please call me next week.

Subjunctive mood is used to express a wish, an opinion, or a hope that is contrary to fact:

If I were in charge, none of this would have happened.

Allison wished she could take the exam over again when she saw her score.

<u>Adjectives</u>

Adjectives are words used to modify nouns and pronouns. They can be used alone or in a series and are used to further define or describe the nouns they modify.

Mark made us a delicious, four-course meal.

The words *delicious* and *four-course* are adjectives that describe the kind of meal Mark made.

Articles are also considered adjectives because they help to describe nouns. Articles can be general or specific. The three articles in English are: a, an, and the.

Indefinite articles (a, an) are used to refer to nonspecific nouns. The article *a* proceeds words beginning with consonant sounds, and the article *an* proceeds words beginning with vowel sounds.

> A car drove by our house.
>
> An alligator was loose at the zoo.
>
> He has always wanted a ukulele. (The first *u* makes a *y* sound.)

Note that *a* and *an* should only proceed nonspecific nouns that are also singular. If a nonspecific noun is plural, it does not need a preceding article.

> Alligators were loose at the zoo.

The *definite article (the)* is used to refer to specific nouns:

> The car pulled into our driveway.

Note that *the* should proceed all specific nouns regardless of whether they are singular or plural.

> The cars pulled into our driveway.

Comparative adjectives are used to compare nouns. When they are used in this way, they take on positive, comparative, or superlative form.

> The positive form is the normal form of the adjective:
>
> > Alicia is tall.
>
> The *comparative* form shows a comparison between two things:
>
> > Alicia is taller than Maria.
>
> *Superlative* form shows comparison between more than two things:
>
> > Alicia is the tallest girl in her class.

Usually, the comparative and superlative can be made by adding *–er* and *–est* to the positive form, but some verbs call for the helping verbs *more* or *most*. Other exceptions to the rule include adjectives like *bad*, which uses the comparative *worse* and the superlative *worst*.

An adjective phrase is not a bunch of adjectives strung together, but a group of words that describes a noun or pronoun and, thus, functions as an adjective. *Very ugly* is an adjective phrase; so are *way too fat* and *faster than a speeding bullet.*

<u>Adverbs</u>

Adverbs have more functions than adjectives because they modify or qualify verbs, adjectives, or other adverbs as well as word groups that express a relation of place, time, circumstance, or cause. Therefore, adverbs answer any of the following questions: *How, when, where, why, in what way, how often, how much, in what condition,* and/or *to what degree. How good looking is he? He is <u>very</u> handsome.*

Here are some examples of adverbs for different situations:

- how: quickly
- when: daily
- where: there
- in what way: easily
- how often: often
- how much: much
- in what condition: badly
- what degree: hardly

As one can see, for some reason, many adverbs end in *-ly.*

Adverbs do things like emphasize (*really, simply,* and *so*), amplify (*heartily, completely,* and *positively*), and tone down (*almost, somewhat,* and *mildly*).

Adverbs also come in phrases.

> *The dog ran as <u>though his life depended on it.</u>*

<u>Prepositions</u>

Prepositions are connecting words and, while there are only about 150 of them, they are used more often than any other individual groups of words. They describe relationships between other words. They are placed before a noun or pronoun, forming a phrase that modifies another word in the sentence. *Prepositional phrases* begin with a preposition and end with a noun or pronoun, the *object of the preposition. A pristine lake is <u>near the store</u> and <u>behind the bank</u>.*

Some commonly used prepositions are *about, after, anti, around, as, at, behind, beside, by, for, from, in, into, of, off, on, to,* and *with.*

Complex prepositions, which also come before a noun or pronoun, consist of two or three words such as *according to, in regards to,* and *because of.*

<u>Conjunctions</u>

Conjunctions are vital words that connect words, phrases, thoughts, and ideas. Conjunctions show relationships between components. There are two types:

Coordinating conjunctions are the primary class of conjunctions placed between words, phrases, clauses, and sentences that are of equal grammatical rank; the coordinating conjunctions are for, and, nor, but, or, yes, and so. A useful memorization trick is to remember that the first letter of these conjunctions collectively spell the word *fanboys*.

> I need to go shopping, *but* I must be careful to leave enough money in the bank.
> She wore a black, red, *and* white shirt.

Subordinating conjunctions are the secondary class of conjunctions. They connect two unequal parts, one *main* (or *independent*) and the other *subordinate* (or *dependent*). I must go to the store *even though* I do not have enough money in the bank.

> *Because* I read the review, I do not want to go to the movie.

Notice that the presence of subordinating conjunctions makes clauses dependent. *I read the review* is an independent clause, but *because* makes the clause dependent. Thus, it needs an independent clause to complete the sentence.

Interjections

Interjections are words used to express emotion. Examples include *wow*, *ouch*, and *hooray*. Interjections are often separate from sentences; in those cases, the interjection is directly followed by an exclamation point. In other cases, the interjection is included in a sentence and followed by a comma. The punctuation plays a big role in the intensity of the emotion that the interjection is expressing. Using a comma or semicolon indicates less excitement than using an exclamation mark..

Subjects

Every sentence must include a subject and a verb. The *subject* of a sentence is who or what the sentence is about. It's often directly stated and can be determined by asking "Who?" or "What?" did the action:

Most sentences contain a direct subject, in which the subject is mentioned in the sentence.

> *Kelly mowed the lawn.*
>
> Who mowed the lawn? *Kelly*
>
> *The air-conditioner ran all night*
>
> What ran all night? *the air-conditioner*

The subject of imperative sentences is *you*, because imperative subjects are commands. the subject is implied because it is a command:

> *Go home after the meeting*.
>
> Who should go home after the meeting? *you* (implied)

In *expletive sentences* that start with "there are" or "there is," the subject is found after the predicate. The subject cannot be "there," so it must be another word in the sentence:

> *There is a cup sitting on the coffee table.*
>
> What is sitting on the coffee table? *a cup*

Simple and Complete Subjects

A *complete subject* includes the simple subject and all the words modifying it, including articles and adjectives. A *simple subject* is the single noun without its modifiers.

> A warm, chocolate-chip cookie sat on the kitchen table.
>
> Complete subject: *a warm, chocolate-chip cookie*
>
> Simple subject: *cookie*

The words *a, warm, chocolate,* and *chip* all modify the simple subject *cookie*.

There might also be a *compound subject*, which would be two or more nouns without the modifiers.

A little girl and her mother walked into the shop.

Complete subject: *A little girl and her mother*

Compound subject: *girl, mother*

In this case, *the girl and her mother* are both completing the action of walking into the shop, so this is a *compound subject*.

<u>Predicates</u>

In addition to the subject, a sentence must also have a predicate. The *predicate* contains a verb and tells something about the subject. In addition to the verb, a predicate can also contain a direct or indirect object, object of a preposition, and other phrases.

The cats napped on the front porch.

In this sentence, *cats* is the subject because they are who or what the sentence is about.

The *complete predicate* is everything else in the sentence: *napped on the front porch.* This phrase is the predicate because it tells us what the cats did.

This sentence can be broken down into a simple subject and predicate:

Cats napped.

In this sentence, *cats* is the simple subject, and *napped* is the *simple predicate*.

Although the sentence is very short and doesn't offer much information, it's still considered a complete sentence because it contains a subject and predicate.

Like a compound subject, a sentence can also have a ***compound predicate***. This is when the subject is or does two or more things in the sentence.

This easy chair reclines and swivels.

In this sentence, *this easy chair* is the complete subject. *Reclines and swivels* shows two actions of the chair, so this is the compound predicate.

<u>Subject-Verb Agreement</u>

The subject of a sentence and its verb must agree. The cornerstone rule of subject-verb agreement is that subject and verb must agree in number. Whether the subject is singular or plural, the verb must follow suit.

Incorrect: The houses is new.
Correct: The houses are new.
Also Correct: The house is new.

In other words, a singular subject requires a singular verb; a plural subject requires a plural verb. The words or phrases that come between the subject and verb do not alter this rule.

Incorrect: The houses built of brick is new.
Correct: The houses built of brick are new.

Incorrect: The houses with the sturdy porches is new.
Correct: The houses with the sturdy porches are new.

The subject will always follow the verb when a sentence begins with *here* or *there.* Identify these with care.

Incorrect: Here *is* the *houses* with sturdy porches.
Correct: Here *are* the *houses* with sturdy porches.

The subject in the sentences above is not *here*, it is *houses*. Remember, *here* and *there* are never subjects. Be careful that contractions such as *here's* or *there're* do not cause confusion!

Two subjects joined by *and* require a plural verb form, except when the two combine to make one thing:

Incorrect: Garrett and Jonathan is over there.
Correct: Garrett and Jonathan are over there.

Incorrect: Spaghetti and meatballs are a delicious meal!
Correct: Spaghetti and meatballs is a delicious meal!

In the example above, *spaghetti and meatballs* is a compound noun. However, *Garrett and Jonathan* is not a compound noun.

Two singular subjects joined by *or, either/or,* or *neither/nor* call for a singular verb form.

Incorrect: Butter or syrup are acceptable.
Correct: Butter or syrup is acceptable.

Plural subjects joined by *or*, *either/or*, or *neither/nor* are, indeed, plural.

The chairs or the boxes are being moved next.

If one subject is singular and the other is plural, the verb should agree with the closest noun.

Correct: The chair or the boxes are being moved next.
Correct: The chairs or the box is being moved next.

Some plurals of money, distance, and time call for a singular verb.

Incorrect: Three dollars *are* enough to buy that.
Correct: Three dollars *is* enough to buy that.

For words declaring degrees of quantity such as *many of, some of,* or *most of,* let the noun that follows *of* be the guide:

> Incorrect: Many of the books is in the shelf.
> Correct: Many of the books are in the shelf.

> Incorrect: Most of the pie *are* on the table.
> Correct: Most of the pie *is* on the table.

For indefinite pronouns like anybody or everybody, use singular verbs.

> Everybody *is* going to the store.

However, the pronouns *few, many, several, all, some,* and *both* have their own rules and use plural forms.

> Some *are* ready.

Some nouns like *crowd* and *congress* are called *collective nouns* and they require a singular verb form.

> Congress *is* in session.
> The news *is* over.

Books and movie titles, though, including plural nouns such as *Great Expectations*, also require a singular verb. Remember that only the subject affects the verb. While writing tricky subject-verb arrangements, say them aloud. Listen to them. Once the rules have been learned, one's ear will become sensitive to them, making it easier to pick out what's right and what's wrong.

<u>Direct Objects</u>

The *direct object* is the part of the sentence that receives the action of the verb. It is a noun and can usually be found after the verb. To find the direct object, first find the verb, and then ask the question *who* or *what* after it.

> The bear climbed the tree.

> What did the bear climb? *the tree*

<u>Indirect Objects</u>

An *indirect object* receives the direct object. It is usually found between the verb and the direct object. A strategy for identifying the indirect object is to find the verb and ask the questions *to whom/for whom* or *to what/ for what*.

> Jane made her daughter a cake.

> For whom did Jane make the cake? *her daughter*

Cake is the direct object because it is what Jane made, and *daughter* is the indirect object because she receives the cake.

Complements

A *complement* completes the meaning of an expression. A complement can be a pronoun, noun, or adjective. A verb complement refers to the direct object or indirect object in the sentence. An object complement gives more information about the direct object:

> The magician got the kids excited.

> *Kids* is the direct object, and *excited* is the object complement.

A *subject complement* comes after a linking verb. It is typically an adjective or noun that gives more information about the subject:

> The king was noble and spared the thief's life.

Noble describes the *king* and follows the linking verb *was*.

Predicate Nouns

A *predicate noun* renames the subject:

> John is a carpenter.

The subject is *John*, and the predicate noun is *carpenter*.

Predicate Adjectives

A *predicate adjective* describes the subject:

> Margaret is beautiful.

The subject is *Margaret*, and the predicate adjective is *beautiful*.

Homonyms

Homonyms are words that sound the same but are spelled differently, and they have different meanings. There are several common homonyms that give writers trouble.

There, They're, and Their

The word *there* can be used as an adverb, adjective, or pronoun:

> *There* are ten children on the swim team this summer.

> I put my book over *there*, but now I can't find it.

The word *they're* is a contraction of the words *they* and *are*:

> *They're* flying in from Texas on Tuesday.

The word *their* is a possessive pronoun:

> I store *their* winter clothes in the attic.

Its and It's

Its is a possessive pronoun:

> The cat licked *its* injured paw.

It's is the contraction for the words *it* and *is*:

> *It's* unbelievable how many people opted not to vote in the last election.

Your and You're
Your is a possessive pronoun:

> Can I borrow *your* lawnmower this weekend?

You're is a contraction for the words *you* and *are*:

> *You're* about to embark on a fantastic journey.

To, Too, and Two
To is an adverb or a preposition used to show direction, relationship, or purpose:

> We are going *to* New York.

> They are going *to* see a show.

Too is an adverb that means more than enough, also, and very:

> You have had *too* much candy.

> We are on vacation that week, *too*.

Two is the written-out form of the numeral 2:

> *Two* of the shirts didn't fit, so I will have to return them.

New and Knew
New is an adjective that means recent:

> There's a *new* customer on the phone.

Knew is the past tense of the verb *know*:

> I *knew* you'd have fun on this ride.

Affect and Effect

Affect and *effect* are complicated because they are used as both nouns and verbs, have similar meanings, and are pronounced the same.

	Affect	**Effect**
Noun Definition	emotional state	result
Noun Example	The patient's affect was flat.	The effects of smoking are well documented.
Verb Definition	to influence	to bring about
Verb Example	The pollen count affects my allergies.	The new candidate hopes to effect change.

Independent and Dependent Clauses

Independent and *dependent* clauses are strings of words that contain both a subject and a verb. An independent clause *can* stand alone as complete thought, but a dependent clause *cannot*. A dependent clause relies on other words to be a complete sentence.

> Independent clause: The keys are on the counter.
> Dependent clause: If the keys are on the counter

Notice that both clauses have a subject (*keys*) and a verb (*are*). The independent clause expresses a complete thought, but the word *if* at the beginning of the dependent clause makes it *dependent* on other words to be a complete thought.

> Independent clause: If the keys are on the counter, please give them to me.

This presents a complete sentence since it includes at least one verb and one subject and is a complete thought. In this case, the independent clause has two subjects (*keys* & an implied *you*) and two verbs (*are* & *give*).

> Independent clause: I went to the store.
> Dependent clause: Because we are out of milk,
>
> Complete Sentence: Because we are out of milk, I went to the store.
> Complete Sentence: I went to the store because we are out of milk.

Phrases

A *phrase* is a group of words that do not make a complete thought or a clause. They are parts of sentences or clauses. Phrases can be used as nouns, adjectives, or adverbs. A phrase does not contain both a subject and a verb.

Prepositional Phrases

A *prepositional phrase* shows the relationship between a word in the sentence and the object of the preposition. The object of the preposition is a noun that follows the preposition.

> The orange pillows are on the couch.

On is the preposition, and *couch* is the object of the preposition.

She brought her friend with the nice car.

With is the preposition, and *car* is the object of the preposition. Here are some common prepositions:

about	as	at	after
by	for	from	in
of	on	to	with

Verbals and Verbal Phrases

Verbals are forms of verbs that act as other parts of speech. They can be used as nouns, adjectives, or adverbs. Though they are use verb forms, they are not to be used as the verb in the sentence. A word group that is based on a verbal is considered a *verbal phrase*. There are three major types of verbals: *participles, gerunds,* and *infinitives.*

Participles are verbals that act as adjectives. The present participle ends in *–ing*, and the past participle ends in *–d, -ed, -n,* or*-t.*

Verb	**Present Participle**	**Past Participle**
walk	walking	walked
share	sharing	shared

Participial phrases are made up of the participle and modifiers, complements, or objects.

Crying for most of an hour, the baby didn't seem to want to nap.

Having already taken this course, the student was bored during class.

Crying for most of an hour and *Having already taken this course* are the participial phrases.

Gerunds are verbals that are used as nouns and end in *–ing*. A gerund can be the subject or object of the sentence like a noun. Note that a present participle can also end in *–ing*, so it is important to distinguish between the two. The gerund is used as a noun, while the participle is used as an adjective.

Swimming is my favorite sport.

I wish I were sleeping.

A *gerund phrase* includes the gerund and any modifiers or complements, direct objects, indirect objects, or pronouns.

Cleaning the house is my least favorite weekend activity.

Cleaning the house is the gerund phrase acting as the subject of the sentence.

The most important goal this year is raising money for charity.

Raising money for charity is the gerund phrase acting as the direct object.

The police accused the woman of stealing the car.

The *gerund* phrase *stealing the car* is the object of the preposition in this sentence.

An *infinitive* is a verbal made up of the word to and a verb. Infinitives can be used as nouns, adjectives, or adverbs.

Examples: To eat, to jump, to swim, to lie, to call, to work

An *infinitive phrase* is made up of the infinitive plus any complements or modifiers. The infinitive phrase *to wait* is used as the subject in this sentence:

To wait was not what I had in mind.

The infinitive phrase *to sing* is used as the subject complement in this sentence:

Her dream is to sing.

The infinitive phrase *to grow* is used as an adverb in this sentence:

Children must eat to grow.

<u>Appositive Phrases</u>

An *appositive* is a noun or noun phrase that renames a noun that comes immediately before it in the sentence. An appositive can be a single word or several words. These phrases can be *essential* or *nonessential*. An essential appositive phrase is necessary to the meaning of the sentence and a nonessential appositive phrase is not. It is important to be able to distinguish these for purposes of comma use.

Essential: My sister Christina works at a school.

Naming which sister is essential to the meaning of the sentence, so no commas are needed.

Nonessential: My sister, who is a teacher, is coming over for dinner tonight.

Who is a teacher is not essential to the meaning of the sentence, so commas are required.

<u>Absolute Phrases</u>

An *absolute phrase* modifies a noun without using a conjunction. It is not the subject of the sentence and is not a complete thought on its own. Absolute phrases are set off from the independent clause with a comma.

Arms outstretched, she yelled at the sky.

All things considered, this has been a great day.

Punctuation

End Punctuation

Periods (.) are used to end a sentence that is a statement (*declarative*) or a command (*imperative*). They should not be used in a sentence that asks a question or is an exclamation. Periods are also used in abbreviations, which are shortened versions of words.

- Declarative: The boys refused to go to sleep.
- Imperative: Walk down to the bus stop.
- Abbreviations: Joan Roberts, M.D., Apple Inc., Mrs. Adamson
- If a sentence ends with an abbreviation, it is inappropriate to use two periods. It should end with a single period after the abbreviation.

The chef gathered the ingredients for the pie, which included apples, flour, sugar, etc.

Question marks (?) are used with direct questions (*interrogative*). An *indirect question* can use a period:

Interrogative: When does the next bus arrive?

Indirect Question: I wonder when the next bus arrives.

An *exclamation point (!)* is used to show strong emotion or can be used as an *interjection*. This punctuation should be used sparingly in formal writing situations.

What an amazing shot!

Whoa!

Commas

A *comma* (,) is the punctuation mark that signifies a pause—breath—between parts of a sentence. It denotes a break of flow. Proper comma usage helps readers understand the writer's intended emphasis of ideas.

In a complex sentence—one that contains a subordinate (dependent) clause or clauses—the use of a comma is dictated by where the subordinate clause is located. If the subordinate clause is located before the main clause, a comma is needed between the two clauses.

I will not pay for the steak, *because I don't have that much money*.

Generally, if the subordinate clause is placed after the main clause, no punctuation is needed. I did well on my exam because I studied two hours the night before. Notice how the last clause is dependent because it requires the earlier independent clauses to make sense.

Use a comma on both sides of an interrupting phrase.

I will pay for the ice cream, chocolate and vanilla, and then will eat it all myself.

The words forming the phrase in italics are nonessential (extra) information. To determine if a phrase is nonessential, try reading the sentence without the phrase and see if it's still coherent.

A comma is not necessary in this next sentence because no interruption—nonessential or extra information—has occurred. Read sentences aloud when uncertain.

I will pay for his chocolate and vanilla ice cream and then will eat it all myself.

If the nonessential phrase comes at the beginning of a sentence, a comma should only go at the end of the phrase. If the phrase comes at the end of a sentence, a comma should only go at the beginning of the phrase.

Other types of interruptions include the following:

- interjections: Oh no, I am not going.
- abbreviations: Barry Potter, M.D., specializes in heart disorders.
- direct addresses: Yes, Claudia, I am tired and going to bed.
- parenthetical phrases: His wife, lovely as she was, was not helpful.
- transitional phrases: Also, it is not possible.

The second comma in the following sentence is called an Oxford comma.

> I will pay for ice cream, syrup, and pop.

It is a comma used after the second-to-last item in a series of three or more items. It comes before the word *or* or *and*. Not everyone uses the Oxford comma; it is optional, but many believe it is needed. The comma functions as a tool to reduce confusion in writing. So, if omitting the Oxford comma would cause confusion, then it's best to include it.

Commas are used in math to mark the place of thousands in numerals, breaking them up so they are easier to read. Other uses for commas are in dates (*March 19, 2016*), letter greetings (*Dear Sally,*), and in between cities and states (*Louisville, KY*).

<u>Semicolons</u>
A *semicolon (;)* is used to connect ideas in a sentence in some way. There are three main ways to use semicolons.

Link two independent clauses without the use of a coordinating conjunction:

> I was late for work again; I'm definitely going to get fired.

Link two independent clauses with a transitional word:

> The songs were all easy to play; therefore, he didn't need to spend too much time practicing.

Between items in a series that are already separated by commas or if necessary to separate lengthy items in a list:

> Starbucks has locations in Media, PA; Swarthmore, PA; and Morton, PA.
>
> Several classroom management issues presented in the study: the advent of a poor teacher persona in the context of voice, dress, and style; teacher follow-through from the beginning of the school year to the end; and the depth of administrative support, including ISS and OSS protocol.

<u>Colons</u>
A *colon* is used after an independent clause to present an explanation or draw attention to what comes next in the sentence. There are several uses.

Explanations of ideas:

> They soon learned the hardest part about having a new baby: sleep deprivation.

Lists of items:

> Shari picked up all the supplies she would need for the party: cups, plates, napkins, balloons, streamers, and party favors.

Time, subtitles, general salutations:

> The time is 7:15.
>
> I read a book entitled *Pluto: A Planet No More*.
>
> To whom it may concern:

Parentheses and Dashes

Parentheses are half-round brackets that look like this: *( )*. They set off a word, phrase, or sentence that is an afterthought, explanation, or side note relevant to the surrounding text but not essential. A pair of commas is often used to set off this sort of information, but parentheses are generally used for information that would not fit well within a sentence or that the writer deems not important enough to be structurally part of the sentence.

> The picture of the heart (see above) shows the major parts you should memorize.
> Mount Everest is one of three mountains in the world that are over 28,000 feet high (K2 and Kanchenjunga are the other two).

See how the sentences above are complete without the parenthetical statements? In the first example, *see above* would not have fit well within the flow of the sentence. The second parenthetical statement could have been a separate sentence, but the writer deemed the information not pertinent to the topic.

The dash (—) is a mark longer than a hyphen used as a punctuation mark in sentences and to set apart a relevant thought. Even after plucking out the line separated by the dash marks, the sentence will be intact and make sense.

> Looking out the airplane window at the landmarks—Lake Clarke, Thompson Community College, and the bridge—she couldn't help but feel excited to be home.

The dashes use is similar to that of parentheses or a pair of commas. So, what's the difference? Many believe that using dashes makes the clause within them stand out while using parentheses is subtler. It's advised to not use dashes when commas could be used instead.

Ellipses

An *ellipsis* (...) consists of three handy little dots that can speak volumes on behalf of irrelevant material. Writers use them in place of a word(s), line, phrase, list contents, or paragraph that might just as easily have been omitted from a passage of writing. This can be done to save space or to focus only on the specifically relevant material.

> Exercise is good for some unexpected reasons. Watkins writes, "Exercise has many benefits such as ...reducing cancer risk."

In the example above, the ellipsis takes the place of the other benefits of exercise that are more expected.

The ellipsis may also be used to show a pause in sentence flow.

> "I'm wondering...how this could happen," Dylan said in a soft voice.

<u>Quotation Marks</u>

Double *quotation marks* are used to at the beginning and end of a direct quote. They are also used with certain titles and to indicate that a term being used is slang or referenced in the sentence. Quotation marks should not be used with an indirect quote. Single quotation marks are used to indicate a quote within a quote.

> Direct quote: "The weather is supposed to be beautiful this week," she said.
>
> Indirect quote: One of the customers asked if the sale prices were still in effect.
>
> Quote within a quote: "My little boy just said 'Mama, I want cookie,'" Maria shared.

Titles: Quotation marks should also be used to indicate titles of short works or sections of larger works, such as chapter titles. Other works that use quotation marks include poems, short stories, newspaper articles, magazine articles, web page titles, and songs.

> "The Road Not Taken" is my favorite poem by Robert Frost.
>
> "What a Wonderful World" is one of my favorite songs.

Specific or emphasized terms: Quotation marks can also be used to indicate a technical term or to set off a word that is being discussed in a sentence. Quotation marks can also indicate sarcasm.

> The new step, called "levigation", is a very difficult technique.
>
> He said he was "hungry" multiple times, but he only ate two bites.

Use with other punctuation: The use of quotation marks with other punctuation varies, depending on the role of the ending or separating punctuation.

In American English, *periods* and *commas* always go inside the quotation marks:

> "This is the last time you are allowed to leave early," his boss stated.
>
> The newscaster said, "We have some breaking news to report."

Question marks or *exclamation points* go inside the quotation marks when they are part of a direct quote:

> The doctor shouted, "Get the crash cart!"

When the question mark or exclamation point is part of the sentence, not the quote, it should be placed outside of the quotation marks:

> Was it Jackie that said, "Get some potatoes at the store"?

Apostrophes

This punctuation mark, the apostrophe (') is a versatile mark. It has several different functions:

- Quotes: Apostrophes are used when a second quote is needed within a quote.
- In my letter to my friend, I wrote, "The girl had to get a new purse, and guess what Mary did? She said, 'I'd like to go with you to the store.' I knew Mary would buy it for her."
- Contractions: Another use for an apostrophe in the quote above is a contraction. I'd is used for I would.
- Possession: An apostrophe followed by the letter s shows possession (Mary's purse). If the possessive word is plural, the apostrophe generally just follows the word. Not all possessive pronouns require apostrophes.
- The trees' leaves are all over the ground.

Hyphens

The *hyphen* (-) is a small hash mark that can be used to join words to show that they are linked.

Hyphenate two words that work together as a single adjective (a compound adjective).

> honey-covered biscuits

Some words always require hyphens, even if not serving as an adjective.

> merry-go-round

Hyphens always go after certain prefixes like *anti-* & *all-*.

Hyphens should also be used when the absence of the hyphen would cause a strange vowel combination (*semi-engineer*) or confusion. For example, *re-collect* should be used to describe something being gathered twice rather than being written as *recollect*, which means to remember.

Practice Questions

Read the selection about travelling in an RV and answer Questions 1-7.

1 I have to admit that when my father bought a recreational vehicle (RV), I thought he was making a huge mistake. I didn't really know anything about RVs, but I knew that my dad was as big a "city slicker" as there was. (1) In fact, I even thought he might have gone a little bit crazy. On trips to the beach, he preferred to swim at the pool, and whenever he went hiking, he avoided touching any plants for fear that they might be poison ivy. Why would this man, with an almost irrational fear of the outdoors, want a 40-foot camping behemoth?

2 (2) The RV was a great purchase for our family and brought us all closer together. Every morning (3) we would wake up, eat breakfast, and broke camp. We laughed at our own comical attempts to back The Beast into spaces that seemed impossibly small. (4) We rejoiced as "hackers." When things inevitably went wrong and we couldn't solve the problems on our own, we discovered the incredible helpfulness and friendliness of the RV community. (5) We even made some new friends in the process.

3 (6) Above all, it allowed us to share adventures. While travelling across America, which we could not have experienced in cars and hotels. Enjoying a campfire on a chilly summer evening with the mountains of Glacier National Park in the background, or waking up early in the morning to see the sun rising over the distant spires of Arches National Park are memories that will always stay with me and our entire family. (7) Those are also memories that my siblings and me have now shared with our own children.

1. Which of the following would be the best choice for this sentence (reproduced below)?

In fact, I even thought he might have gone a little bit crazy.

a. Leave it where it is now.
b. Move the sentence so that it comes before the preceding sentence.
c. Move the sentence to the end of the first paragraph.
d. Omit the sentence.

2. In context, which is the best version of the underlined portion of this sentence (reproduced below)?

The RV was a great purchase for our family and brought us all closer together.

a. (as it is now)
b. Not surprisingly, the RV
c. Furthermore, the RV
d. As it turns out, the RV

3. Which is the best version of the underlined portion of this sentence (reproduced below)?

Every morning *we would wake up, eat breakfast, and broke camp.*

a. (as it is now)
b. we would wake up, eat breakfast, and break camp.
c. would we wake up, eat breakfast, and break camp?
d. we are waking up, eating breakfast, and breaking camp.

4. Which is the best version of the underlined portion of this sentence (reproduced below)?

We rejoiced as "hackers."

a. (as it is now)
b. To a nagging problem of technology, we rejoiced as "hackers."
c. We rejoiced when we figured out how to "hack" a solution to a nagging technological problem.
d. To "hack" our way to a solution, we had to rejoice.

5. Which is the best version of the underlined portion of this sentence (reproduced below)?

We even made some new friends in the process.

a. (as it is now)
b. In the process was the friends we were making.
c. We are even making some new friends in the process.
d. We will make new friends in the process.

6. Which is the best version of the underlined portion of this sentence (reproduced below)?

Above all, it allowed us to share adventures. While travelling across America, which we could not have experienced in cars and hotels.

a. (as it is now)
b. Above all, it allowed us to share adventures while traveling across America
c. Above all, it allowed us to share adventures; while traveling across America
d. Above all, it allowed us to share adventures—while traveling across America

7. Which is the best version of the underlined portion of this sentence (reproduced below)?

Those are also memories that my siblings and me have now shared with our own children.

a. (as it is now)
b. Those are also memories that me and my siblings
c. Those are also memories that my siblings and I
d. Those are also memories that I and my siblings

Read the following section about Fred Hampton and answer Questions 8-20.

1 Fred Hampton desired to see lasting social change for African American people through nonviolent means and community recognition. (8) <u>In the meantime,</u> he became an African American activist during the American Civil Rights Movement and led the Chicago chapter of the Black Panther Party.

Hampton's Education

2 Hampton was born and raised (9) <u>in Maywood of Chicago, Illinois in 1948.</u> Gifted academically and a natural athlete, he became a stellar baseball player in high school. (10) <u>After graduating from Proviso East High School in 1966, he later went on to study law at Triton Junior College. While studying at Triton, Hampton joined and became a leader of the National Association for the Advancement of Colored People (NAACP). As a result of his leadership, the NAACP gained more than 500 members.</u> Hampton worked relentlessly to acquire recreational facilities in the neighborhood and improve the educational resources provided to the impoverished black community of Maywood.

The Black Panthers

3 The Black Panther Party (BPP) (11) <u>was another that</u> formed around the same time as and was similar in function to the NAACP. Hampton was quickly attracted to the (12) <u>Black Panther Party's approach</u> to the fight for equal rights for African Americans. Hampton eventually joined the chapter and relocated to downtown Chicago to be closer to its headquarters.

4 His charismatic personality, organizational abilities, sheer determination, and rhetorical skills (13) <u>enable him to quickly rise</u> through the chapter's ranks. Hampton soon became the leader of the Chicago chapter of the BPP where he organized rallies, taught political education classes, and established a free medical clinic. (14) <u>He also took part in the community police supervision project. He played an instrumental role</u> in the BPP breakfast program for impoverished African American children.

5 Hampton's (15) <u>greatest</u> <u>acheivement</u> as the <u>leader</u> of the BPP may be his fight against street gang violence in Chicago. In 1969, (16) <u>Hampton was held by a press conference</u> where he made the gangs agree to a nonaggression pact known as the Rainbow Coalition. As a result of the pact, a multiracial alliance between blacks, Puerto Ricans, and poor youth was developed.

Assassination

6 (17) <u>As the Black Panther Party's popularity and influence grew, the Federal Bureau of Investigation (FBI) placed the group under constant surveillance.</u> In an attempt to neutralize the party, the FBI launched several harassment campaigns against the BPP, raided its headquarters in Chicago three times, and arrested over one hundred of the group's members. Hampton was shot during such a raid that occurred on the morning of December 4th 1969.

7 (18) <u>In 1976; seven years after the event,</u> it was revealed that William O'Neal, Hampton's trusted bodyguard, was an undercover FBI agent. (19) <u>O'Neal will provide</u> the FBI with detailed floor plans of the BPP's headquarters, identifying the exact location of Hampton's bed. It was because of these floor plans that the police were able to target and kill Hampton.

8 The assassination of Hampton fueled outrage amongst the African American community. It was not until years after the assassination that the police admitted wrongdoing. (20) The Chicago City Council now are commemorating December 4th as Fred Hampton Day.

8. In context, which is the best version of the underlined portion of this sentence (reproduced below)?

In the meantime, he became an African American activist during the American Civil Rights Movement and led the Chicago chapter of the Black Panther Party.

a. (as it is now)
b. Unfortunately,
c. Finally,
d. As a result,

9. Which is the best version of the underlined portion of this sentence (reproduced below)?

Hampton was born and raised in Maywood of Chicago, Illinois in 1948.

a. (as it is now)
b. in Maywood, of Chicago, Illinois in 1948.
c. in Maywood of Chicago, Illinois, in 1948.
d. in Chicago, Illinois of Maywood in 1948.

10. Which of the following sentences, if any, should begin a new paragraph?

After graduating from Proviso East High School in 1966, he later went on to study law at Triton Junior College. While studying at Triton, Hampton joined and became a leader of the National Association for the Advancement of Colored People (NAACP). As a result of his leadership, the NAACP gained more than 500 members.

a. There should be no new paragraph.
b. After graduating from Proviso East High School in 1966, he later went on to study law at Triton Junior College.
c. While studying at Triton, Hampton joined and became a leader of the National Association for the Advancement of Colored People (NAACP).
d. As a result of his leadership, the NAACP gained more than 500 members.

11. Which of the following facts would be the most relevant to include here?

The Black Panther Party (BPP) was another that formed around the same time as and was similar in function to the NAACP.

a. best as written
b. was another activist group that
c. had a lot of members that
d. was another school that

12. Which is the best version of the underlined portion of this sentence (reproduced below)?

Hampton was quickly attracted to the Black Panther Party's approach to the fight for equal rights for African Americans.

a. (as it is now)
b. Black Panther Parties approach
c. Black Panther Partys' approach
d. Black Panther Parties' approach

13. Which is the best version of the underlined portion of this sentence (reproduced below)?

His charismatic personality, organizational abilities, sheer determination, and rhetorical skills enable him to quickly rise through the chapter's ranks.

a. (as it is now)
b. are enabling him to quickly rise
c. enabled him to quickly rise
d. will enable him to quickly rise

14. Which is the best version of the underlined portion of this sentence (reproduced below)?

He also took part in the community police supervision project. He played an instrumental role in the BPP breakfast program for impoverished African American children.

a. (as it is now)
b. He also took part in the community police supervision project but played an instrumental role
c. He also took part in the community police supervision project, he played an instrumental role
d. He also took part in the community police supervision project and played an instrumental role

15. Which of these, if any, is misspelled?

Hampton's (15) greatest acheivement as the leader of the BPP may be his fight against street gang violence in Chicago.

a. None of these are misspelled.
b. greatest
c. acheivement
d. leader

16. Which is the best version of the underlined portion of this sentence (reproduced below)?

In 1969, Hampton was held by a press conference where he made the gangs agree to a nonaggression pact known as the Rainbow Coalition.

a. (as it is now)
b. Hampton held a press conference
c. Hampton, holding a press conference
d. Hampton to hold a press conference

17. Which is the best version of the underlined portion of this sentence (reproduced below)?

As the Black Panther Party's popularity and influence grew, the Federal Bureau of Investigation (FBI) placed the group under constant surveillance.

a. (as it is now)
b. The Federal Bureau of Investigation (FBI) placed the group under constant surveillance as the Black Panther Party's popularity and influence grew.
c. Placing the group under constant surveillance, the Black Panther Party's popularity and influence grew.
d. As their influence and popularity grew, the FBI placed the group under constant surveillance.

18. Which is the best version of the underlined portion of this sentence (reproduced below)?

In 1976; seven years after the event, it was revealed that William O'Neal, Hampton's trusted bodyguard, was an undercover FBI agent.

a. (as it is now)
b. In 1976, seven years after the event,
c. In 1976 seven years after the event,
d. In 1976. Seven years after the event,

19. Which is the best version of the underlined portion of this sentence (reproduced below)?

O'Neal will provide the FBI with detailed floor plans of the BPP's headquarters, identifying the exact location of Hampton's bed.

a. (as it is now)
b. O'Neal provides
c. O'Neal provided
d. O'Neal, providing

20. Which is the best version of the underlined portion of this sentence (reproduced below)?

The Chicago City Council now are commemorating December 4th as Fred Hampton Day.

a. (as it is now)
b. Fred Hampton Day by the Chicago City Council, December 4, is now commemorated.
c. Now commemorated December 4th is Fred Hampton Day.
d. The Chicago City Council now commemorates December 4th as Fred Hampton Day.

Read the following passage and answer Questions 21-25.

1 Although many Missourians know that Harry S. Truman and Walt Disney hailed from their great state, probably far fewer know that it was also home to the remarkable George Washington Carver. (21) As a child, George was driven to learn, and he loved painting. At the end of the Civil War, Moses Carver, the slave owner who owned George's parents, decided to keep George and his brother and raise them on his farm.

2 He even went on to study art while in college but was encouraged to pursue botany instead. He spent much of his life helping others (22) by showing them better ways to farm, his ideas improved agricultural productivity in many countries. One of his most notable contributions to the newly emerging class of Negro farmers was to teach them the negative effects of agricultural monoculture, i.e. (23) growing the same crops in the same fields year after year, depleting the soil of much needed nutrients and results in a lesser yielding crop.

3 Carver was an innovator, always thinking of new and better ways to do things, and is most famous for his over three hundred uses for the peanut. Toward the end of his career, (24) Carver returns to his first love of art. Through his artwork, he hoped to inspire people to see the beauty around them and to do great things themselves. (25) Because Carver died, he left his money to help fund ongoing agricultural research. Today, people still visit and study at the George Washington Carver Foundation at Tuskegee Institute.

21. Which of the following would be the best choice for this sentence (reproduced below)?

As a child, George was driven to learn, and he loved painting.

a. Leave it as it is now
b. Move to the end of the first paragraph.
c. Move to the beginning of the first paragraph.
d. Move to the end of the second paragraph.

22. Which is the best version of the underlined portion of this sentence (reproduced below)?

He spent much of his life helping others by showing them better ways to farm, his ideas improved agricultural productivity in many countries.

a. (as it is now)
b. by showing them better ways to farm his ideas improved agricultural productivity
c. by showing them better ways to farm . . . his ideas improved agricultural productivity
d. by showing them better ways to farm; his ideas improved agricultural productivity

23. Which is the best version of the underlined portion of this sentence (reproduced below)?

One of his most notable contributions to the newly emerging class of Negro farmers was to teach them the negative effects of agricultural monoculture, i.e. growing the same crops in the same fields year after year, depleting the soil of much needed nutrients and results in a lesser yielding crop.

a. (as it is now)
b. growing the same crops in the same fields year after year, depleting the soil of much needed nutrients and resulting in a lesser yielding crop.
c. growing the same crops in the same fields year after year, depletes the soil of much needed nutrients and resulting in a lesser yielding crop.
d. grows the same crops in the same fields year after year, depletes the soil of much needed nutrients and resulting in a lesser yielding crop.

24. In context, which is the best version of the underlined portion of this sentence (reproduced below)?

Toward the end of his career, Carver returns to his first love of art.

a. (as it is now)
b. Carver is returning
c. Carver returned
d. Carver was returning

25. In context, which is the best version of the underlined portion of this sentence (reproduced below)?

Because Carver died, he left his money to help fund ongoing agricultural research.

a. (as it is now)
b. Although Carver died,
c. When Carver died,
d. Finally Carver died,

Answer Explanations

1. B: Move the sentence so that it comes before the preceding sentence. For this question, place the underlined sentence in each prospective choice's position. To keep as-is is incorrect because the father "going crazy" doesn't logically follow the fact that he was a "city slicker." Choice *C* is incorrect because the sentence in question is not a concluding sentence, and does not transition smoothly into the second paragraph. Choice *D* is incorrect because the sentence doesn't necessarily need to be omitted since it logically follows the very first sentence in the passage.

2. D: Choice *D* is correct because "As it turns out" indicates a contrast from the previous sentiment, that the RV was a great purchase. Choice *A* is incorrect because the sentence needs an effective transition from the paragraph before. Choice *B* is incorrect because the text indicates it *is* surprising that the RV was a great purchase because the author was skeptical beforehand. Choice *C* is incorrect because the transition "Furthermore" does not indicate a contrast.

3. B: This sentence calls for parallel structure. Choice *B* is correct because the verbs "wake," "eat," and "break" are consistent in tense and parts of speech. Choice *A* is incorrect because the words "wake" and "eat" are present tense while the word "broke" is in past tense. Choice *C* is incorrect because this turns the sentence into a question, which doesn't make sense within the context. Choice *D* is incorrect because it breaks tense with the rest of the passage. "Waking," "eating," and "breaking" are all present participles, and the context around the sentence is in past tense.

4. C: Choice *C* is correct because it is clear, concise, and fits within the context of the passage. Choice *A* is incorrect because "We rejoiced as 'hackers'" does not give reason *why* hacking was rejoiced. Choice *B* is incorrect because it does not mention a solution being found and is therefore not specific enough. Choice *D* is incorrect because the meaning is eschewed by the helping verb "had to rejoice," and the sentence does not give enough detail as to what the problem entails.

5. A: The original sentence is correct because the verb tense as well as the order of the sentence makes sense in the given context. Choice *B* is incorrect because the order of the words makes the sentence more confusing than it otherwise would be. Choice *C* is incorrect because "We are even making" is in present tense. Choice *D* is incorrect because "We will make" is future tense. The surrounding text of the sentence is in past tense.

6. B: Choice *B* is correct because there is no punctuation needed if a dependent clause ("while traveling across America") is located behind the independent clause ("it allowed us to share adventures"). Choice *A* is incorrect because there are two dependent clauses connected and no independent clause, and a complete sentence requires at least one independent clause. Choice *C* is incorrect because of the same reason as Choice *A*. Semicolons have the same function as periods: there must be an independent clause on either side of the semicolon. Choice *D* is incorrect because the dash simply interrupts the complete sentence.

7. C: The rules for "me" and "I" is that one should use "I" when it is the subject pronoun of a sentence, and "me" when it is the object pronoun of the sentence. Break the sentence up to see if "I" or "me" should be used. To say "Those are memories that I have now shared" makes more sense than to say "Those are memories that me have now shared." Choice *D* is incorrect because "my siblings" should come before "I."

8. D: Choice *D* is correct because Fred Hampton becoming an activist was a direct result of him wanting to see lasting social change for African American people. Choice *A* doesn't make sense because "In the meantime" denotes something happening at the same time as another thing. Choice *B* is incorrect because the text's tone does not indicate that becoming a civil rights activist is an unfortunate path. Choice *C* is incorrect because "Finally" indicates something that comes last in a series of events, and the word in question is at the beginning of the introductory paragraph.

9. A: Choice *A* is correct because there should be a comma between the city and state. Choice *B* is incorrect because the comma after "Maywood" interrupts the phrase "Maywood of Chicago." Choice *C* is incorrect because a comma after "Illinois" is unnecessary. Finally, Choice *D* is incorrect because the order of the sentence designates that Chicago, Illinois is in Maywood, which is incorrect.

10. C: This is a difficult question. The paragraph is incorrect as-is because it is too long and thus loses the reader halfway through. Choice *C* is correct because if the new paragraph began with "While studying at Triton," we would see a smooth transition from one paragraph to the next. We can also see how the two paragraphs are logically split in two. The first half of the paragraph talks about where he studied. The second half of the paragraph talks about the NAACP and the result of his leadership in the association. If we look at the passage as a whole, we can see that there are two main topics that should be broken in two.

11. B: The BPP is another activist group. We can figure out this answer by looking at context clues. We know that the BPP is "similar in function" to the NAACP. To find out what the NAACP's function is, we must look at the previous sentences. We know from above that the NAACP is an activist group, so we can assume that the BPP is also an activist group.

12. A: Choice *A* is correct because the Black Panther Party is one entity, therefore the possession should show the "Party's approach" with the apostrophe between the "y" and the "s." Choice *B* is incorrect because the word "Parties" should not be plural. Choice *C* is incorrect because the apostrophe indicates that the word "Partys" is plural. The plural of "party" is "parties." Choice *D* is incorrect because, again, the word "parties" should not be plural; instead, it is one unified party.

13. C: Choice *C* is correct because the passage is told in past tense, and "enabled" is a past tense verb. Choice *A,* "enable," is present tense. Choice *B*, "are enabling," is a present participle, which suggests a continuing action. Choice *D*, "will enable," is future tense.

14. D: Choice *D* is correct because the conjunction "and" is the best way to combine the two independent clauses. Choice *A* is incorrect because the word "he" becomes repetitive since the two clauses can be joined together. Choice *B* is incorrect because the conjunction "but" indicates a contrast, and there is no contrast between the two clauses. Choice *C* is incorrect because the introduction of the comma after "project" with no conjunction creates a comma splice.

15. C: The word "acheivement" is misspelled. Remember the rules for "*i* before *e* except after *c*." Choices *B* and *D*, "greatest" and "leader," are both spelled correctly.

16. B: Choice *B* is correct because it provides the correct verb tense and also makes sense within the context of the passage. Choice *A* is incorrect because it doesn't make sense for someone to be "held by a press conference." Choice *C* is incorrect because, with this use of the sentence, it would create a fragment because the verb "holding" has no helping verb in front of it. Choice *D* is incorrect because it adds an infinitive ("to hold") where a past tense form of a verb should be.

17. A: Choice *A* is correct because it provides the most clarity. Choice *B* is incorrect because it doesn't name the group until the end, so the phrase "the group" is vague. Choice *C* is incorrect because it indicates that the BPP's popularity grew as a result of placing the group under constant surveillance, which is incorrect. Choice *D* is incorrect because there is a misplaced modifier; this sentence actually says that the FBI's influence and popularity grew, which is incorrect.

18. B: Choice *B* is correct. Choice *A* is incorrect because there should be an independent clause on either side of a semicolon, and the phrase "In 1976" is not an independent clause. Choice *C* is incorrect because there should be a comma after introductory phrases in general, such as "In 1976," and Choice *C* omits a comma. Choice *D* is incorrect because the sentence "In 1976." is a fragment.

19. C: Choice *C* is correct because the past tense verb "provided" fits in with the rest of the verb tense throughout the passage. Choice *A*, "will provide," is future tense. Choice *B*, "provides," is present tense. Choice *D*, "providing," is a present participle, which means the action is continuous.

20. D: The correct answer is Choice *D* because this statement provides the most clarity. Choice *A* is incorrect because the noun "Chicago City Council" acts as one, so the verb "are" should be singular, not plural. Choice *B* is incorrect because it is perhaps the most confusingly worded out of all the answer choices; the phrase "December 4" interrupts the sentence without any indication of purpose. Choice *C* is incorrect because it is too vague and leaves out *who* does the commemorating.

21. B: The best place for this sentence given all the answer choices is at the end of the first paragraph. Choice *A* is incorrect; the passage is told in chronological order, and leaving the sentence as-is defies that order, since we haven't been introduced to who raised George. Choice *C* is incorrect because this sentence is not an introductory sentence. It does not provide the main topic of the paragraph. Choice *D* is incorrect because again, it defies chronological order. By the end of paragraph two we have already gotten to George as an adult, so this sentence would not make sense here.

22. D: Out of these choices, a semicolon would be the best fit because there is an independent clause on either side of the semicolon, and the two sentences closely relate to each other. Choice *A* is incorrect because putting a comma between two independent clauses (i.e. complete sentences) creates a comma splice. Choice *B* is incorrect; omitting punctuation here creates a run-on sentence. Choice *C* is incorrect because an ellipses (. . .) is used to designate an omission in the text.

23. B: This is another instance of parallel structure. Choice *A* is incorrect because the verbs in the original sentence are "growing," "depleting," and "results," the last of which has a different form than the first two. Choices *C* and *D* add "depletes" and "grows," both of which abandon the "-ing" verbs.

24. C: Choice *C* is correct because it keeps with the verb tense in the rest of the passage: past tense. Choice *A* is in present tense, which is incorrect. Choice *B* is present progressive, which means there is a continual action, which is also incorrect. Choice *D* is incorrect because "was returning" is past progressive tense, which means that something was happening continuously at some point in the past.

25. C: The correct choice is the subordinating conjunction, "When." We should look at the clues around the phrase to see what fits best. Carver left his money "when he died." Choice *A*, "Because," could perhaps be correct, but "When" is the more appropriate word to use here. Choice *B* is incorrect; "Although" denotes a contrast, and there is no contrast here. Choice *D* is incorrect because "Finally" indicates something at the very end of a list or series, and there is no series at this point in the text.

Arithmetic

Whole Number and Fraction Operations

Addition with Whole Numbers and Fractions

Addition combines two quantities together. With whole numbers, this is taking two sets of things and merging them into one, then counting the result. For example, 4 + 3 = 7. When adding numbers, the order does not matter: 3 + 4 = 7, also. Longer lists of whole numbers can also be added together. The result of adding numbers is called the *sum*.

With fractions, the number on top is the *numerator*, and the number on the bottom is the *denominator*. To add fractions, the denominator must be the same—a *common denominator*. To find a common denominator, the existing numbers on the bottom must be considered, and the lowest number they will both multiply into must be determined. Consider the following equation:

$$\frac{1}{3}+\frac{5}{6}=?$$

The numbers 3 and 6 both multiply into 6. Three can be multiplied by 2, and 6 can be multiplied by 1. The top and bottom of each fraction must be multiplied by the same number. Then, the numerators are added together to get a new numerator. The following equation is the result:

$$\frac{1}{3}+\frac{5}{6}=\frac{2}{6}+\frac{5}{6}=\frac{7}{6}$$

Subtraction with Whole Numbers and Fractions

Subtraction is taking one quantity away from another, so it is the opposite of addition. The expression 4 – 3 means taking 3 away from 4. So, 4 – 3 = 1. In this case, the order matters, since it entails taking one quantity away from the other, rather than just putting two quantities together. The result of subtraction is also called the *difference*.

To subtract fractions, the denominator must be the same. Then, subtract the numerators together to get a new numerator. Here is an example:

$$\frac{1}{3}-\frac{5}{6}=\frac{2}{6}-\frac{5}{6}=\frac{-3}{6}=-\frac{1}{2}$$

Multiplication with Whole Numbers and Fractions

Multiplication is a kind of repeated addition. The expression 4×5 is taking four sets, each of them having five things in them, and putting them all together. That means $4 \times 5 = 5 + 5 + 5 + 5 = 20$. As with addition, the order of the numbers does not matter. The result of a multiplication problem is called the *product.*

To multiply fractions, the numerators are multiplied to get the new numerator, and the denominators are multiplied to get the new denominator:

$$\frac{1}{3}\times\frac{5}{6}=\frac{1\times 5}{3\times 6}=\frac{5}{18}$$

When multiplying fractions, common factors can *cancel* or *divide into one another*, when factors that appear in the numerator of one fraction and the denominator of the other fraction. Here is an example:

$$\frac{1}{3} \times \frac{9}{8} = \frac{1}{1} \times \frac{3}{8} = 1 \times \frac{3}{8} = \frac{3}{8}$$

The numbers 3 and 9 have a common factor of 3, so that factor can be divided out.

Division with Whole Numbers and Fractions

Division is the opposite of multiplication. With whole numbers, it means splitting up one number into sets of equal size. For example, $16 \div 8$ is the number of sets of eight things that can be made out of sixteen things. Thus, $16 \div 8 = 2$. As with subtraction, the order of the numbers will make a difference, here. The answer to a division problem is called the *quotient*, while the number in front of the division sign is called the *dividend* and the number behind the division sign is called the *divisor*.

To divide fractions, the first fraction must be multiplied with the reciprocal of the second fraction. The *reciprocal* of the fraction $\frac{x}{y}$ is the fraction $\frac{y}{x}$. Here is an example:

$$\frac{1}{3} \div \frac{5}{6} = \frac{1}{3} \times \frac{6}{5} = \frac{6}{15} = \frac{2}{5}$$

Decimal Operations

Recognition of Decimals

The *decimal system* is a way of writing out numbers that uses ten different numerals: 0, 1, 2, 3, 4, 5, 6, 7, 8, and 9. This is also called a "base ten" or "base 10" system. Other bases are also used. For example, computers work with a base of 2. This means they only use the numerals 0 and 1.

The *decimal place* denotes how far to the right of the decimal point a numeral is. The first digit to the right of the decimal point is in the *tenths* place. The next is the *hundredths*. The third is the *thousandths*.

So, 3.142 has a 1 in the tenths place, a 4 in the hundredths place, and a 2 in the thousandths place.

The *decimal point* is a period used to separate the *ones* place from the *tenths* place when writing out a number as a decimal.

A *decimal number* is a number written out with a decimal point instead of as a fraction, for example, 1.25 instead of $\frac{5}{4}$. Depending on the situation, it can sometimes be easier to work with fractions and sometimes easier to work with decimal numbers.

A decimal number is *terminating* if it stops at some point. It is called *repeating* if it never stops, but repeats a pattern over and over. It is important to note that every rational number can be written as a terminating decimal or as a repeating decimal.

Addition with Decimals

To add decimal numbers, each number in columns needs to be lined up by the decimal point. For each number being added, the zeros to the right of the last number need to be filled in so that each of the numbers has the same number of places to the right of the decimal. Then, the columns can be added together. Here is an example of 2.45 + 1.3 + 8.891 written in column form:

2.450

1.300

+ 8.891

Zeros have been added in the columns so that each number has the same number of places to the right of the decimal.

Added together, the correct answer is 12.641:

2.450

1.300

+ 8.891

12.641

Subtraction with Decimals

Subtracting decimal numbers is the same process as adding decimals. Here is 7.89 – 4.235 written in column form:

7.890

- 4.235

3.655

A zero has been added in the column so that each number has the same number of places to the right of the decimal.

Multiplication with Decimals

Decimals can be multiplied as if there were no decimal points in the problem. For example, 0.5 x 1.25 can be rewritten and multiplied as 5 x 125, which equals 625.

The final answer will have the same number of decimal *points* as the total number of decimal *places* in the problem. The first number has one decimal place, and the second number has two decimal places. Therefore, the final answer will contain three decimal places:

0.5 x 1.25 = 0.625

Division with Decimals

Dividing a decimal by a whole number entails using long division first by ignoring the decimal point. Then, the decimal point is moved the number of places given in the problem.

For example, $6.8 \div 4$ can be rewritten as $68 \div 4$, which is 17. There is one non-zero integer to the right of the decimal point, so the final solution would have one decimal place to the right of the solution. In this case, the solution is 1.7.

Dividing a decimal by another decimal requires changing the divisor to a whole number by moving its decimal point. The decimal place of the dividend should be moved by the same number of places as the divisor. Then, the problem is the same as dividing a decimal by a whole number.

For example, $5.72 \div 1.1$ has a divisor with one decimal point in the denominator. The expression can be rewritten as $57.2 \div 11$ by moving each number one decimal place to the right to eliminate the decimal. The long division can be completed as $572 \div 11$ with a result of 52. Since there is one non-zero integer to the right of the decimal point in the problem, the final solution is 5.2.

In another example, $8 \div 0.16$ has a divisor with two decimal points in the denominator. The expression can be rewritten as $800 \div 16$ by moving each number two decimal places to the right to eliminate the decimal in the divisor. The long division can be completed with a result of 50.

Percent

The word *percent* comes from the Latin phrase for "per one hundred." A *percent* is a way of writing out a fraction. It is a fraction with a denominator of 100. Thus, $65\% = \frac{65}{100}$.

To convert a fraction to a percent, the denominator is written as 100. For example, $\frac{3}{5} = \frac{60}{100} = 60\%$.

In converting a percent to a fraction, the percent is written with a denominator of 100, and the result is simplified. For example, $30\% = \frac{30}{100} = \frac{3}{10}$.

Percent Problems

The basic percent equation is the following:

$$\frac{is}{of} = \frac{\%}{100}$$

The placement of numbers in the equation depends on what the question asks.

Example 1
Find 40% of 80.

Basically, the problem is asking, "What is 40% of 80?" The 40% is the percent, and 80 is the number to find the percent "of." The equation is:

$$\frac{x}{80} = \frac{40}{100}$$

Solving the equation by cross-multiplication, the problem becomes 100x = 80(40). Solving for x gives the answer: x = 32.

Example 2
What percent of 100 is 20?

The 20 fills in the "is" portion, while 100 fills in the "of." The question asks for the percent, so that will be x, the unknown. The following equation is set up:

$$\frac{20}{100} = \frac{x}{100}$$

Cross-multiplying yields the equation 100x = 20(100). Solving for x gives the answer of 20%.

Example 3
30% of what number is 30?

The following equation uses the clues and numbers in the problem:

$$\frac{30}{x} = \frac{30}{100}$$

Cross-multiplying results in the equation 30(100) = 30x. Solving for x gives the answer x = 100.

Number Comparisons and Equivalents

Recognizing Equivalent Fractions and Mixed Numbers

The value of a fraction does not change if multiplying or dividing both the numerator and the denominator by the same number (other than 0). In other words, $\frac{x}{y} = \frac{a\times x}{a\times y} = \frac{x\div a}{y\div a}$, as long as *a* is not 0. This means that $\frac{2}{5} = \frac{4}{10}$, for example. If *x* and *y* are integers that have no common factors, then the fraction is said to be *simplified*. This means $\frac{2}{5}$ is simplified, but $\frac{4}{10}$ is not.

Often when working with fractions, the fractions need to be rewritten so that they all share a single denominator—this is called finding a *common denominator* for the fractions. Using two fractions, $\frac{a}{b}$ and $\frac{c}{d}$, the numerator and denominator of the left fraction can be multiplied by *d*, while the numerator and denominator of the right fraction can be multiplied by *b*. This provides the fractions $\frac{a\times d}{b\times d}$ and $\frac{c\times b}{d\times b}$ with the common denominator $b \times d$.

A fraction whose numerator is smaller than its denominator is called a *proper fraction*. A fraction whose numerator is bigger than its denominator is called an *improper fraction*. These numbers can be rewritten as a combination of integers and fractions, called a *mixed number*. For example, $\frac{6}{5} = \frac{5}{5} + \frac{1}{5} = 1 + \frac{1}{5}$, and can be written as $1\frac{1}{5}$.

Estimating

Estimation is finding a value that is close to a solution but is not the exact answer. For example, if there are values in the thousands to be multiplied, then each value can be estimated to the nearest thousand and the calculation performed. This value provides an approximate solution that can be determined very quickly.

Ordering of Numbers

In counting, when a number appears after another number in order, that number will be one more. On the other hand, when a number appears before another number in order, that number will be one less. This idea is useful when counting backward. Also, zero means that there is none of something. This idea can be seen by taking away all of something so that there are zero items left. Also, learning to count by tens starting at any number is a key concept. Once a new number is learned, learning how to read and write that number is also important.

Placing numbers in an order in which they are listed from smallest to largest is known as *ordering*. When items are listed by using numbers in order, the *ordinal numbers*, 1st, 2nd, 3rd, 4th, ..., can be used.

When you order numbers the right way, you can more easily compare the different amounts of items. When you compare numbers you show whether two amounts are the same or different. Teachers can show two different quantities of items in the classroom. Then they can discuss which amount is lesser or greater. This exercise also can be used in order to classify numbers from the smallest amount to the largest amount.

Being able to compare any two whole numbers without a visual representation is also an important task. Each whole number relates to a certain amount. This amount can be ranked and compared to other amounts. Knowing the right vocabulary relating to ordering and comparing is important. The *equals sign* is $=$. It shows that two numbers are the same on either side of the symbol. For example, $28 = 28$. The symbols that are used for comparison are $<$ to represent *less than*, $>$ to represent *greater than*. The symbols $\leq$ to represent *less than or equal to*, and $\geq$ to represent *greater than or equal to*, and $\neq$ to represent *not equal to* can also be used.

You can compare numbers with any number of digits when you use these symbols. For example, the expression $77 < 100$, should be understood as 77 is less than 100. The expression $44 > 23$ should be understood as 44 is greater than 23. The expression $22 \neq 24$ should be understood as 22 is not equal *to 24*. Also, both $36 = 36$ and $36 \leq 36$ can be written because both "36 equals 36" and "36 is less than or equal to 36" applies.

<u>Patterns</u>

Patterns are an important part of mathematics. When mathematical calculations are completed repeatedly, patterns can be recognized. Recognizing patterns is an integral part of mathematics because it helps you understand relationships between different ideas. For example, a sequence of numbers can be given, and being able to recognize the relationship between the given numbers can help in completing the sequence.

For instance, given the sequence of numbers $7, 14, 21, 28, 35, \ldots$, the next number in the sequence would be 42. This is because the sequence lists all multiples of 7, starting at 7. Sequences can also be built from addition, subtraction, and division. Being able to recognize the relationship between the values that are given is the key to finding out the next number in the sequence.

Patterns within a sequence can come in 2 distinct forms. The items either repeat in a constant order, or the items change from one step to another in some consistent way. The core is the smallest unit, or number of items, that repeats in a repeating pattern. For example, the pattern ○○▲○○▲○... has a core that is ○○▲. Knowing only the core, the pattern can be extended. Knowing the number of steps in the core allows the identification of an item in each step without drawing/writing the entire pattern out. For example, suppose you must find the tenth item in the previous pattern. Because the core consists of three items (○○▲), the core repeats in multiples of 3. In other words, steps 3, 6, 9, 12, etc. will be ▲ completing the core with the core starting over on the next step. For the above example, the 9th step will be ▲ and the 10th will be ○.

The most common patterns where each item changes from one step to the next are arithmetic and geometric sequences. In an arithmetic sequence, the items increase or decrease by a constant difference. In other words, the same thing is added or subtracted to each item or step to produce the next. To determine if a sequence is arithmetic, see what must be added or subtracted to step one to produce step two. Then, check if the same thing is added/subtracted to step two to produce step three. The same thing must be added/subtracted to step three to produce step four, and so on. Consider the pattern 13, 10, 7, 4, … . To get from step one (13) to step two (10) by adding or subtracting requires subtracting by 3. The next step is checking if subtracting 3 from step two (10) will produce step three (7), and subtracting 3 from step three (7) will produce step four (4). In this case, the pattern holds true. Therefore, this is an arithmetic sequence in which each step is produced by subtracting 3 from the previous step. To extend the sequence, 3 is subtracted from the last step to produce the next. The next three numbers in the sequence are 1, -2, -5.

A geometric sequence is one in which each step is produced by multiplying or dividing the previous step by the same number. To see if a sequence is geometric, decide what step one must be multiplied or divided by to produce step two. Then check if multiplying or dividing step two by the same number produces step three, and so on. Consider the pattern 2, 8, 32, 128, … . To get from step one (2) to step two (8) requires multiplication by 4. The next step determines if multiplying step two (8) by 4 produces step three (32), and multiplying step three (32) by 4 produces step four (128). In this case, the pattern holds true. Therefore, this is a geometric sequence in which each step is found by multiplying the previous step by 4. To extend the sequence, the last step is multiplied by 4 and repeated. The next three numbers in the sequence are 512; 2,048; 8,192.

Arithmetic and geometric sequences can also be represented by shapes. For example, an arithmetic sequence could consist of shapes with three sides, four sides, and five sides. A geometric sequence could consist of eight blocks, four blocks, and two blocks (each step is produced by dividing the number of blocks in the previous step by 2).

Relationships Between the Corresponding Terms of Two Numerical Patterns

When given two number patterns, the corresponding terms should be examined to determine if a relationship exists between them. Corresponding terms between patterns are the pairs of numbers which appear in the same step of the two sequences. Consider the following patterns 1, 2, 3, 4,… and 3, 6, 9, 12, … . The corresponding terms are: 1 and 3; 2 and 6; 3 and 9; and 4 and 12. To identify the relationship, each pair of corresponding terms is examined. You can also examine the possibilities of performing an operation (+, −, ×, ÷) to each sequence. In this case:

$$1 + 2 = 3 \text{ or } 1 \times 3 = 3$$

$$2 + 4 = 6 \text{ or } 2 \times 3 = 6$$

$$3 + 6 = 9 \text{ or } 3 \times 3 = 9$$

$$4 + 8 = 12 \text{ or } 4 \times 3 = 12$$

The pattern is that the number from the first sequence multiplied by 3 equals the number in the second sequence. By assigning each sequence a label (input and output) or variable (x and y), the relationship can be written as an equation. The first sequence represents the inputs, or *x*, and the second sequence represents the outputs, or *y*. So, the relationship can be expressed as: $y = 3x$.

Consider the following sets of numbers:

a	2	4	6	8
b	6	8	10	12

To write a rule for the relationship between the values for *a* and the values for *b*, the corresponding terms (2 and 6; 4 and 8; 6 and 10; 8 and 12) are examined. The possibilities for producing *b* from *a* are:

$2 + 4 = 6 \text{ or } 2 \times 3 = 6$

$4 + 4 = 8 \text{ or } 4 \times 2 = 8$

$6 + 4 = 10$

$8 + 4 = 12 \text{ or } 8 \times 1.5 = 12$

The pattern is that adding 4 to the value of *a* produces the value of *b*. The relationship can be written as the equation $a + 4 = b$.

Practice Questions

1. $3.4 + 2.35 + 4 =$
   a. 5.35
   b. 9.2
   c. 9.75
   d. 10.25

2. $5.88 \times 3.2 =$
   a. 18.816
   b. 16.44
   c. 20.352
   d. 17

3. $\frac{3}{25} =$
   a. 0.15
   b. 0.1
   c. 0.9
   d. 0.12

4. Which of the following is largest?
   a. 0.45
   b. 0.096
   c. 0.3
   d. 0.313

5. Which of the following is NOT a way to write 40 percent of *N*?
   a. $(0.4)N$
   b. $\frac{2}{5}N$
   c. $40N$
   d. $\frac{4N}{10}$

6. Which is closest to 17.8×9.9?
   a. 140
   b. 180
   c. 200
   d. 350

7. A student gets an 85% on a test with 20 questions. How many answers did the student solve correctly?
   a. 15
   b. 16
   c. 17
   d. 18

8. Four people split a bill. The first person pays for $\frac{1}{5}$, the second person pays for $\frac{1}{4}$, and the third person pays for $\frac{1}{3}$. What fraction of the bill does the fourth person pay?

a. $\frac{13}{60}$

b. $\frac{47}{60}$

c. $\frac{1}{4}$

d. $\frac{4}{15}$

9. 6 is 30% of what number?

a. 18

b. 20

c. 24

d. 26

10. $3\frac{2}{3} - 1\frac{4}{5} =$

a. $1\frac{13}{15}$

b. $\frac{14}{15}$

c. $2\frac{2}{3}$

d. $\frac{4}{5}$

11. What is $\frac{420}{98}$ rounded to the nearest integer?

a. 4

b. 3

c. 5

d. 6

12. $4\frac{1}{3} + 3\frac{3}{4} =$

a. $6\frac{5}{12}$

b. $8\frac{1}{12}$

c. $8\frac{2}{3}$

d. $7\frac{7}{12}$

13. Five of six numbers have a sum of 25. The average of all six numbers is 6. What is the sixth number?

a. 8

b. 10

c. 11

d. 12

14. $52.3 \times 10^{-3} =$

a. 0.00523

b. 0.0523

c. 0.523

d. 523

15. If $\frac{5}{2} \div \frac{1}{3} = n$, then n is between:

a. 5 and 7

b. 7 and 9

c. 9 and 11

d. 3 and 5

16. A closet is filled with red, blue, and green shirts. If $\frac{1}{3}$ of the shirts are green and $\frac{2}{5}$ are red, what fraction of the shirts are blue?

a. $\frac{4}{15}$

b. $\frac{1}{5}$

c. $\frac{7}{15}$

d. $\frac{1}{2}$

17. Shawna buys $2\frac{1}{2}$ gallons of paint. If she uses $\frac{1}{3}$ of it on the first day, how much does she have left?

a. $1\frac{5}{6}$ gallons

b. $1\frac{1}{2}$ gallons

c. $1\frac{2}{3}$ gallons

d. 2 gallons

18. A rectangle has a length that is 5 feet longer than three times its width. If the perimeter is 90 feet, what is the length in feet?

a. 10

b. 20

c. 25

d. 35

19. Five students take a test. The scores of the first four students are 80, 85, 75, and 60. If the median score is 80, which of the following could NOT be the score of the fifth student?

a. 60

b. 80

c. 85

d. 100

20. In an office, there are 50 workers. A total of 60% of the workers are women, and the chances of a woman wearing a skirt is 50%. If no men wear skirts, how many workers are wearing skirts?

a. 12
b. 15
c. 16
d. 20

Answer Explanations

1. C: The decimal points are lined up, with zeroes put in as needed. Then, the numbers are added just like integers:

$$\begin{array}{r} 3.40 \\ 2.35 \\ +\underline{4.00} \\ 9.75 \end{array}$$

2. A: This problem can be multiplied as 588×32, except at the end, the decimal point needs to be moved three places to the left. Performing the multiplication will give 18,816, and moving the decimal place over three places results in 18.816.

3. D: The fraction is converted so that the denominator is 100 by multiplying the numerator and denominator by 4, to get $\frac{3}{25} = \frac{12}{100}$. Dividing a number by 100 just moves the decimal point two places to the left, with a result of 0.12.

4. A: Figure out which is largest by looking at the first non-zero digits. Choice *B*'s first non-zero digit is in the hundredths place. The other three all have non-zero digits in the tenths place, so it must be *A*, *C*, or *D*. Of these, *A* has the largest first non-zero digit.

5. C: 40*N* would be 4000% of *N*. It's possible to check that each of the others is actually 40% of *N*.

6. B: Instead of multiplying these out, the product can be estimated by using $18 \times 10 = 180$. The error here should be lower than 15, since it is rounded to the nearest integer, and the numbers add to something less than 30.

7. C: 85% of a number means multiplying that number by 0.85. So, $0.85 \times 20 = \frac{85}{100} \times \frac{20}{1}$, which can be simplified to $\frac{17}{20} \times \frac{20}{1} = 17$.

8. A: To find the fraction of the bill that the first three people pay, the fractions need to be added, which means finding common denominator. The common denominator will be 60.

$$\frac{1}{5} + \frac{1}{4} + \frac{1}{3} = \frac{12}{60} + \frac{15}{60} + \frac{20}{60} = \frac{47}{60}$$

The remainder of the bill is:

$$1 - \frac{47}{60} = \frac{60}{60} - \frac{47}{60} = \frac{13}{60}$$

9. B: 30% is 3/10. The number itself must be 10/3 of 6, or $\frac{10}{3} \times 6 = 10 \times 2 = 20$.

10. A: These numbers to improper fractions: $\frac{11}{3} - \frac{9}{5}$. Take 15 as a common denominator:

$\frac{11}{3} - \frac{9}{5} =: \frac{55}{15} - \frac{27}{15} = \frac{28}{15} = 1\frac{13}{15}$ (when rewritten to get rid of the partial fraction)

11. A: Dividing by 98 can be approximated by dividing by 100, which would mean shifting the decimal point of the numerator to the left by 2. The result is 4.2 and rounds to 4.

12. B:

$$4\frac{1}{3} + 3\frac{3}{4} = 4 + 3 + \frac{1}{3} + \frac{3}{4} = 7 + \frac{1}{3} + \frac{3}{4}$$

Adding the fractions gives:

$$\frac{1}{3} + \frac{3}{4} = \frac{4}{12} + \frac{9}{12} = \frac{13}{12} = 1 + \frac{1}{12}$$

Thus:

$$7 + \frac{1}{3} + \frac{3}{4} = 7 + 1 + \frac{1}{12} = 8\frac{1}{12}$$

13. C: The average is calculated by adding all six numbers, then dividing by 6. The first five numbers have a sum of 25. If the total divided by 6 is equal to 6, then the total itself must be 36. The sixth number must be 36 – 25 = 11.

14. B: Multiplying by 10^{-3} means moving the decimal point three places to the left, putting in zeroes as necessary.

15. B:

$$\frac{5}{2} \div \frac{1}{3} = \frac{5}{2} \times \frac{3}{1} = \frac{15}{2} = 7.5$$

16. A: The total fraction taken up by green and red shirts will be:

$$\frac{1}{3} + \frac{2}{5} = \frac{5}{15} + \frac{6}{15} = \frac{11}{15}$$

The remaining fraction is:

$$1 - \frac{11}{15} = \frac{15}{15} - \frac{11}{15} = \frac{4}{15}$$

17. C: If she has used 1/3 of the paint, she has 2/3 remaining. $2\frac{1}{2}$ gallons are the same as $\frac{5}{2}$ gallons. The calculation is:

$$\frac{2}{3} \times \frac{5}{2} = \frac{5}{3} = 1\frac{2}{3}\text{ gallons}$$

18. D: Denote the width as *w* and the length as *l*. Then, $l = 3w + 5$. The perimeter is $2w + 2l = 90$. Substituting the first expression for *l* into the second equation yields $2(3w + 5) + 2w = 90$, or $8w = 80$, so$w = 10$. Putting this into the first equation, it yields $l = 3(10) + 5 = 35$.

19. A: Lining up the given scores provides the following list: 60, 75, 80, 85, and one unknown. Because the median needs to be 80, it means 80 must be the middle data point out of these five. Therefore, the unknown data point must be the fourth or fifth data point, meaning it must be greater than or equal to 80. The only answer that fails to meet this condition is 60.

20. B: If 60% of 50 workers are women, then there are 30 women working in the office. If half of them are wearing skirts, then that means 15 women wear skirts. Since none of the men wear skirts, this means there are 15 people wearing skirts.

Quantitative Reasoning, Algebra, and Statistics (QAS)

Rational Numbers

Computation with Integers and Negative Rational Numbers

Integers are the whole numbers together with their negatives. They include numbers like 5, 24, 0, -6, and 15. They do not include fractions or numbers that have digits after the decimal point.

Rational numbers are all numbers that can be written as a fraction using integers. A *fraction* is written as $\frac{x}{y}$ and represents the quotient of *x* being divided by *y*. More practically, it means dividing the whole into *y* equal parts, then taking *x* of those parts.

Examples of rational numbers include $\frac{1}{2}$ and $\frac{5}{4}$. The number on the top is called the *numerator*, and the number on the bottom is called the *denominator*. Because every integer can be written as a fraction with a denominator of 1, (e.g. $\frac{3}{1} = 3$), every integer is also a rational number.

When adding integers and negative rational numbers, there are some basic rules to determine if the solution is negative or positive:

Adding two positive numbers results in a positive number: 3.3 + 4.8 = 8.1.

Adding two negative numbers results in a negative number: (-8) + (-6) = -14.

Adding one positive and one negative number requires taking the absolute values and finding the difference between them. Then, the sign of the number that has the higher absolute value for the final solution is used.

For example, (-9) + 11, has a difference of absolute values of 2. The final solution is 2 because 11 has the higher absolute value. Another example is 9 + (-11), which has a difference of absolute values of 2. The final solution is -2 because 11 has the higher absolute value.

When subtracting integers and negative rational numbers, one has to change the problem to adding the opposite and then apply the rules of addition.

Subtracting two positive numbers is the same as adding one positive and one negative number.

For example, 4.9 – 7.1 is the same as 4.9 + (-7.1). The solution is -2.2 since the absolute value of -7.1 is greater. Another example is 8.5 – 6.4 which is the same as 8.5 + (-6.4). The solution is 2.1 since the absolute value of 8.5 is greater.

Subtracting a positive number from a negative number results in negative value.

For example, (-12) – 7 is the same as (-12) + (-7) with a solution of -19.

Subtracting a negative number from a positive number results in a positive value.

For example, 12 – (-7) is the same as 12 + 7 with a solution of 19.

For multiplication and division of integers and rational numbers, if both numbers are positive or both numbers are negative, the result is a positive value.

For example, (-1.7)(-4) has a solution of 6.8 since both numbers are negative values.

If one number is positive and another number is negative, the result is a negative value.

For example, (-15)/5 has a solution of -3 since there is one negative number.

Ratio and Proportional Relationships

A *ratio* compares the size of one group to the size of another. For example, there may be a room with 4 tables and 24 chairs. The ratio of tables to chairs is $4:24$. Such ratios behave like fractions in that both sides of the ratio by the same number can be multiplied or divided. Thus, the ratio 4:24 is the same as the ratio 2:12 and 1:6.

One quantity is *proportional* to another quantity if the first quantity is always some multiple of the second. For instance, the distance travelled in five hours is always five times to the speed as travelled. The distance is proportional to speed in this case.

One quantity is *inversely proportional* to another quantity if the first quantity is equal to some number divided by the second quantity. The time it takes to travel one hundred miles will be given by 100 divided by the speed travelled. The time is inversely proportional to the speed.

When dealing with word problems, there is no fixed series of steps to follow, but there are some general guidelines to use. It is important that the quantity to be found is identified. Then, it can be determined how the given values can be used and manipulated to find the final answer.

*Ratio*s are used to show the relationship between two quantities. The ratio of oranges to apples in the grocery store may be 3 to 2. That means that for every 3 oranges, there are 2 apples. This comparison can be expanded to represent the actual number of oranges and apples. Another example may be the number of boys to girls in a math class. If the ration of boys to girls is given as 2 to 5, that means there are 2 boys to every 5 girls in the class. Ratios can also be compared if the units in each ratio are the same. The ratio of boys to girls in the math class can be compared to the ratio of boys to girls in a science class by stating which ratio is higher and which is lower.

Rates are used to compare two quantities with different units. *Unit rates* are the simplest form of rate. With unit rates, the denominator in the comparison of two units is one. For example, if someone can type at a rate of 1000 words in 5 minutes, then his or her unit rate for typing is $\frac{1000}{5} = 200$ words in one minute or 200 words per minute. Any rate can be converted into a unit rate by dividing to make the denominator one. 1000 words in 5 minutes has been converted into the unit rate of 200 words per minute.

Ratios and rates can be used together to convert rates into different units. For example, if someone is driving 50 kilometers per hour, that rate can be converted into miles per hour by using a ratio known as the *conversion factor*. Since the given value contains kilometers and the final answer needs to be in miles, the ratio relating miles to kilometers needs to be used. There are 0.62 miles in 1 kilometer.

This, written as a ratio and in fraction form, is:

$$\frac{0.62\ miles}{1\ km}$$

To convert 50km/hour into miles per hour, the following conversion needs to be set up:

$$\frac{50\ km}{hour} * \frac{0.62\ miles}{1\ km} = 31\ miles\ per\ hour$$

The ratio between two similar geometric figures is called the *scale factor*. For example, a problem may depict two similar triangles, A and B. The scale factor from the smaller triangle A to the larger triangle B is given as 2 because the length of the corresponding side of the larger triangle, 16, is twice the corresponding side on the smaller triangle, 8. This scale factor can also be used to find the value of a missing side, x, in triangle A. Since the scale factor from the smaller triangle (A) to larger one (B) is 2, the larger corresponding side in triangle B (given as 25), can be divided by 2 to find the missing side in A ($x =$ 12.5). The scale factor can also be represented in the equation $2A = B$ because two times the lengths of A gives the corresponding lengths of B. This is the idea behind similar triangles.

Much like a scale factor can be written using an equation like $2A = B$, a *relationship* is represented by the equation $Y = kX$. X and Y are proportional because as values of X increase, the values of Y also increase. A relationship that is inversely proportional can be represented by the equation $Y = \frac{k}{X}$, where the value of Y decreases as the value of x increases and vice versa.

Proportional reasoning can be used to solve problems involving ratios, percentages, and averages. Ratios can be used in setting up proportions and solving them to find unknowns. For example, if a student completes an average of 10 pages of math homework in 3 nights, how long would it take the student to complete 22 pages? Both ratios can be written as fractions. The second ratio would contain the unknown.

The following proportion represents this problem, where x is the unknown number of nights:

$$\frac{10\ pages}{3\ nights} = \frac{22\ pages}{x\ nights}$$

Solving this proportion entails cross-multiplying and results in the following equation: $10x = 22 * 3$. Simplifying and solving for x results in the exact solution: $x = 6.6\ nights$. The result would be rounded up to 7 because the homework would actually be completed on the 7th night.

The following problem uses ratios involving percentages:

If 20% of the class is girls and 30 students are in the class, how many girls are in the class?

To set up this problem, it is helpful to use the common proportion:

$$\frac{\%}{100} = \frac{is}{of}$$

Within the proportion, % is the percentage of girls, 100 is the total percentage of the class, *is* is the number of girls, and *of* is the total number of students in the class. Most percentage problems can be written using this language. To solve this problem, the proportion should be set up as $\frac{20}{100} = \frac{x}{30}$, and then solved for x. Cross-multiplying results in the equation $20 * 30 = 100x$, which results in the solution $x = 6$. There are 6 girls in the class.

Problems involving volume, length, and other units can also be solved using ratios. A problem may ask for the volume of a cone to be found that has a radius, $r = 7m$ and a height, $h = 16m$. Referring to the formulas provided on the test, the volume of a cone is given as:

$$V = \pi r^2 \frac{h}{3}$$

r is the radius, and h is the height. Plugging $r = 7$ and $h = 16$ into the formula, the following is obtained:

$$V = \pi(7^2)\frac{16}{3}$$

Therefore, volume of the cone is found to be approximately 821m^3. Sometimes, answers in different units are sought. If this problem wanted the answer in liters, 821m^3 would need to be converted.

Using the equivalence statement $1\text{m}^3 = 1000\text{L}$, the following ratio would be used to solve for liters:

$$821\text{m}^3 * \frac{1000L}{1m^3}$$

Cubic meters in the numerator and denominator cancel each other out, and the answer is converted to 821,000 liters, or $8.21 * 10^5$ L.

Other conversions can also be made between different given and final units. If the temperature in a pool is 30°C, what is the temperature of the pool in degrees Fahrenheit? To convert these units, an equation is used relating Celsius to Fahrenheit. The following equation is used:

$$T_{°F} = 1.8T_{°C} + 32$$

Plugging in the given temperature and solving the equation for T yields the result:

$$T_{°F} = 1.8(30) + 32 = 86°F$$

Both units in the metric system and U.S. customary system are widely used.

Example 1

Jana wants to travel to visit Alice, who lives one hundred and fifty miles away. If she can drive at fifty miles per hour, how long will her trip take?

The quantity to find is the *time* of the trip. The time of a trip is given by the distance to travel divided by the speed to be traveled. The problem determines that the distance is one hundred and fifty miles, while the speed is fifty miles per hour. Thus, 150 divided by 50 is $150 \div 50 = 3$. Because *miles* and *miles per hour* are the units being divided, the miles cancel out. The result is 3 hours.

Example 2

Bernard wishes to paint a wall that measures twenty feet wide by eight feet high. It costs ten cents to paint one square foot. How much money will Bernard need for paint?

The final quantity to compute is the *cost* to paint the wall. This will be ten cents ($0.10) for each square foot of area needed to paint. The area to be painted is unknown, but the dimensions of the wall are given; thus, it can be calculated.

The dimensions of the wall are 20 feet wide and 8 feet high. Since the area of a rectangle is length multiplied by width, the area of the wall is 8 x 20 = 160 square feet. Multiplying 0.1 x 160 yields $16 as the cost of the paint.

The *average* or *mean* of a collection of numbers is given by adding those numbers together and then dividing by the total number of values. A *weighted average* or *weighted mean* is given by adding the numbers multiplied by their weights, then dividing by the sum of the weights:

$$\frac{w_1x_1 + w_2x_2 + w_3x_3 \ldots + w_nx_n}{w_1 + w_2 + w_3 + \cdots + w_n}$$

An *ordinary average* is a weighted average where all the weights are 1.

Exponents

Properties of Exponents

Exponents are used in mathematics to express a number or variable multiplied by itself a certain number of times. For example, x^3 means *x* is multiplied by itself three times. In this expression, x is called the *base*, and 3 is the *exponent*. Exponents can be used in more complex problems when they contain fractions and negative numbers.

Fractional exponents can be explained by looking first at the inverse of exponents, which are *roots*. Given the expression x^2, the square root can be taken, $\sqrt{x^2}$, cancelling out the 2 and leaving *x* by itself, if *x* is positive. Cancellation occurs because $\sqrt{x}$ can be written with exponents, instead of roots, as $x^{\frac{1}{2}}$. The numerator of 1 is the exponent, and the denominator of 2 is called the root (which is why it's referred to as *square root*). Taking the square root of x^2 is the same as raising it to the $\frac{1}{2}$ power. Written out in mathematical form, it takes the following progression:

$$\sqrt{x^2} = (x^2)^{\frac{1}{2}} = x$$

From properties of exponents, $2 \times \frac{1}{2} = 1$ is the actual exponent of *x*. Another example can be seen with $x^{\frac{4}{7}}$. The variable *x*, raised to four-sevenths, is equal to the seventh root of *x* to the fourth power: $\sqrt[7]{x^4}$. In general,

$$x^{\frac{1}{n}} = \sqrt[n]{x}$$

and

$$x^{\frac{m}{n}} = \sqrt[n]{x^m}$$

Negative exponents also involve fractions. Whereas y^3 can also be rewritten as $\frac{y^3}{1}$, y^{-3} can be rewritten as $\frac{1}{y^3}$. A negative exponent means the exponential expression must be moved to the opposite spot in a fraction to make the exponent positive. If the negative appears in the numerator, it moves to the denominator. If the negative appears in the denominator, it is moved to the numerator. In general, $a^{-n} = \frac{1}{a^n}$, and a^{-n} and a^n are reciprocals.

Take, for example, the following expression:

$$\frac{a^{-4}b^2}{c^{-5}}$$

Since *a* is raised to the negative fourth power, it can be moved to the denominator. Since *c* is raised to the negative fifth power, it can be moved to the numerator. The *b* variable is raised to the positive second power, so it does not move.

The simplified expression is as follows:

$$\frac{b^2c^5}{a^4}$$

In mathematical expressions containing exponents and other operations, the order of operations must be followed. *PEMDAS* states that exponents are calculated after any parenthesis and grouping symbols, but before any multiplication, division, addition, and subtraction.

The Evaluation of Positive Rational Roots and Exponents

There are a few rules for working with exponents. For any numbers a, b, m, n, the following hold true:

$$a^1 = a$$

$$1^a = 1$$

$$a^0 = 1$$

$$a^m \times a^n = a^{m+n}$$

$$a^m \div a^n = a^{m-n}$$

$$(a^m)^n = a^{m \times n}$$

$$(a \times b)^m = a^m \times b^m$$

$$(a \div b)^m = a^m \div b^m$$

Any number, including a fraction, can be an exponent. The same rules apply.

Algebraic Expressions

Algebraic expressions look similar to equations, but they do not include the equal sign. Algebraic expressions are comprised of numbers, variables, and mathematical operations. Some examples of algebraic expressions are $8x + 7y - 12z$, $3a^2$, and $5x^3 - 4y^4$.

Algebraic expressions and equations can be used to represent real-life situations and model the behavior of different variables. For example, $2x + 5$ could represent the cost to play games at an arcade. In this case, 5 represents the price of admission to the arcade and 2 represents the cost of each game played. To calculate the total cost, use the number of games played for x, multiply it by 2, and add 5.

Rewriting Expressions

Expressions can be rewritten based on their factors. For example, the expression $6x + 4$ can be rewritten as $2(3x + 2)$ because 2 is a factor of both $6x$ and 4. More complex expressions can also be rewritten based on their factors. The expression $x^4 - 16$ can be rewritten as $(x^2 - 4)(x^2 + 4)$. This is a different type of factoring, where a difference of squares is factored into a sum and difference of the same two terms. With some expressions, the factoring process is simple and only leads to a different way to represent the expression. With others, factoring and rewriting the expression leads to more information about the given problem.

In the following quadratic equation, factoring the binomial leads to finding the zeros of the function:

$$x^2 - 5x + 6 = y$$

This equations factors into $(x - 3)(x - 2) = y$, where 2 and 3 are found to be the zeros of the function when y is set equal to zero. The zeros of any function are the x-values where the graph of the function on the coordinate plane crosses the x-axis.

Factoring an equation is a simple way to rewrite the equation and find the zeros, but factoring is not possible for every quadratic. Completing the square is one way to find zeros when factoring is not an option. The following equation cannot be factored: $x^2 + 10x - 9 = 0$. The first step in this method is to move the constant to the right side of the equation, making it $x^2 + 10x = 9$. Then, the coefficient of x is divided by 2 and squared. This number is then added to both sides of the equation, to make the equation still true. For this example, $\left(\frac{10}{2}\right)^2 = 25$ is added to both sides of the equation to obtain:

$$x^2 + 10x + 25 = 9 + 25$$

This expression simplifies to $x^2 + 10x + 25 = 34$, which can then be factored into $(x + 5)^2 = 34$. Solving for x then involves taking the square root of both sides and subtracting 5. This leads to two zeros of the function:

$$x = \pm\sqrt{34} - 5$$

Depending on the type of answer the question seeks, a calculator may be used to find exact numbers.

Given a quadratic equation in standard form— $ax^2 + bx + c = 0$—the sign of a tells whether the function has a minimum value or a maximum value. If $a > 0$, the graph opens up and has a minimum value. If $a < 0$, the graph opens down and has a maximum value. Depending on the way the quadratic equation is written, multiplication may need to occur before a max/min value is determined.

Exponential expressions can also be rewritten, just as quadratic equations. Properties of exponents must be understood. Multiplying two exponential expressions with the same base involves adding the exponents:

$$a^m a^n = a^{m+n}$$

Dividing two exponential expressions with the same base involves subtracting the exponents:

$$\frac{a^m}{a^n} = a^{m-n}$$

Raising an exponential expression to another exponent includes multiplying the exponents:

$$(a^m)^n = a^{mn}$$

The zero power always gives a value of 1: $a^0 = 1$. Raising either a product or a fraction to a power involves distributing that power:

$$(ab)^m = a^m b^m \text{ and } \left(\frac{a}{b}\right)^m = \frac{a^m}{b^m}$$

Finally, raising a number to a negative exponent is equivalent to the reciprocal including the positive exponent:

$$a^{-m} = \frac{1}{a^m}$$

Linear Equations

A function is called *linear* if it can take the form of the equation $f(x) = ax + b$, or $y = ax + b$, for any two numbers *a* and *b*. A linear equation forms a straight line when graphed on the coordinate plane. An example of a linear function is shown below on the graph.

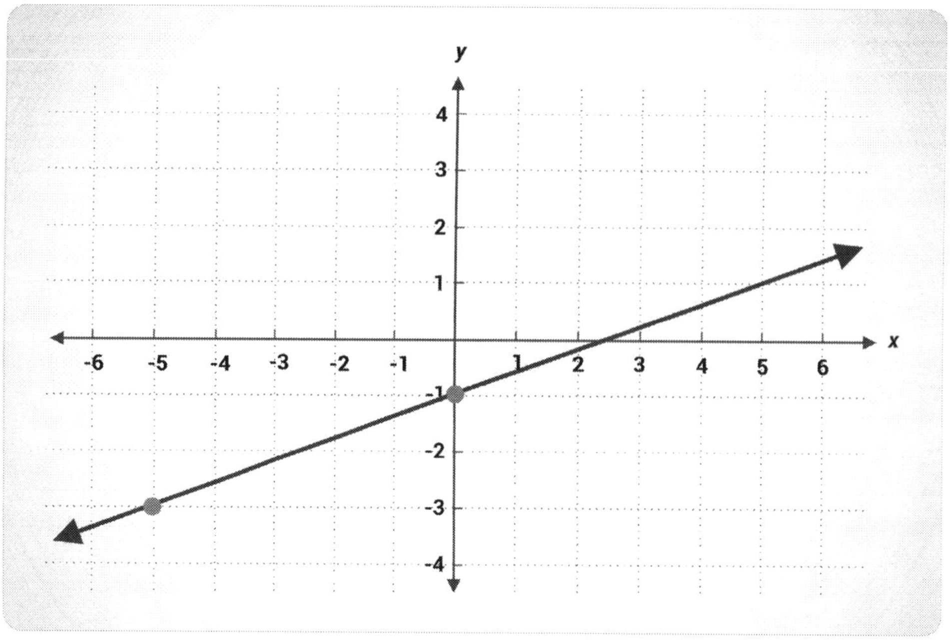

This is a graph of the following function: $y = \frac{2}{5}x - 1$. A table of values that satisfies this function is shown below.

x	y
-5	-3
0	-1
5	1
10	3

These points can be found on the graph using the form (x,y). For more on graphing in the coordinate plane, refer to the Graphing section below.

Forms of Linear Equations

When graphing a linear function, note that the ratio of the change of the *y* coordinate to the change in the *x* coordinate is constant between any two points on the resulting line, no matter which two points are chosen. In other words, in a pair of points on a line, (x_1, y_1) and (x_2, y_2), with $x_1 \neq x_2$ so that the two points are distinct, then the ratio $\frac{y_2-y_1}{x_2-x_1}$ will be the same, regardless of which particular pair of points are chosen. This ratio, $\frac{y_2-y_1}{x_2-x_1}$, is called the *slope* of the line and is frequently denoted with the letter m. If slope *m* is positive, then the line goes upward when moving to the right, while if slope *m* is negative, then the line goes downward when moving to the right. If the slope is 0, then the line is called *horizontal*, and the *y* coordinate is constant along the entire line. In lines where the *x* coordinate is constant along the entire line, *y* is not actually a function of *x*. For such lines, the slope is not defined. These lines are called *vertical* lines.

Linear functions may take forms other than $y = ax + b$. The most common forms of linear equations are explained below:

- Standard Form: $\mathrm{Ax + By = C}$, in which the slope is given by $\mathrm{m} = \frac{-\mathrm{A}}{\mathrm{B}}$, and the y-intercept is given by $\frac{\mathrm{C}}{\mathrm{B}}$.
- Slope-Intercept Form: $\mathrm{y = mx + b}$, where the slope is m and the y intercept is b.
- Point-Slope Form: $\mathrm{y - y_1 = m(x - x_1)}$, where the slope is m and $(\mathrm{x_1, y_1})$ is any point on the chosen line.
- Two-Point Form: $\frac{\mathrm{y-y_1}}{\mathrm{x-x_1}} = \frac{\mathrm{y_2-y_1}}{\mathrm{x_2-x_1}}$, where $(\mathrm{x_1, y_1})$ and $(\mathrm{x_2, y_2})$ are any two distinct points on the chosen line. Note that the slope is given by $\mathrm{m} = \frac{\mathrm{y_2-y_1}}{\mathrm{x_2-x_1}}$.
- Intercept Form: $\frac{\mathrm{x}}{\mathrm{x_1}} + \frac{\mathrm{y}}{\mathrm{y_1}} = 1$, in which $\mathrm{x_1}$ is the x-intercept and $\mathrm{y_1}$ is the y-intercept.

These five ways to write linear equations are all useful in different circumstances. Depending on the given information, it may be easier to write one of the forms over another.

If $y = mx$, y is directly proportional to x. In this case, changing x by a factor changes y by that same factor. If $y = \frac{m}{x}$, y is inversely proportional to x. For example, if x is increased by a factor of 3, then y will be decreased by the same factor, 3.

Solving Linear Equations

Sometimes, rather than a situation where there's an equation such as $y = ax + b$ and finding y for some value of x is requested, the result is given and finding x is requested.

The key to solving any equation is to remember that from one true equation, another true equation can be found by adding, subtracting, multiplying, or dividing both sides by the same quantity. In this case, it's necessary to manipulate the equation so that one side only contains x. Then the other side will show what x is equal to.

For example, in solving $3x - 5 = 2$, adding 5 to each side results in $3x = 7$. Next, dividing both sides by 3 results in $x = \frac{7}{3}$. To ensure the value of x is correct, the number can be substituted into the original equation and solved to see if it makes a true statement. For example, $3(\frac{7}{3}) - 5 = 2$ can be simplified by cancelling out the two 3s. This yields $7 - 5 = 2$, which is a true statement.

Sometimes an equation may have more than one x term. For example, consider the following equation:

$$3x + 2 = x - 4$$

Moving all of the x terms to one side by subtracting x from both sides results in:

$$2x + 2 = -4$$

Next, subtract 2 from both sides so that there is no constant term on the left side. This yields $2x = -6$. Finally, divide both sides by 2, which leaves $x = -3$.

Systems of Equations

A *system of equations* is a group of equations that have the same variables or unknowns. These equations can be linear, but they are not always so. Finding a solution to a system of equations means finding the values of the variables that satisfy each equation. For a linear system of two equations and two variables, there could be a single solution, no solution, or infinitely many solutions.

A single solution occurs when there is one value for x and y that satisfies the system. This would be shown on the graph where the lines cross at exactly one point. When there is no solution, the lines are parallel and do not ever cross. With infinitely many solutions, the equations may look different, but they are the same line. One equation will be a multiple of the other, and on the graph, they lie on top of each other.

The process of elimination can be used to solve a system of equations. For example, the following equations make up a system:

$$x + 3y = 10 \text{ and } 2x - 5y = 9$$

Immediately adding these equations does not eliminate a variable, but it is possible to change the first equation by multiplying the whole equation by -2.

This changes the first equation to:

$$-2x - 6y = -20$$

The equations can be then added to obtain $-11y = -11$. Solving for y yields $y = 1$. To find the rest of the solution, 1 can be substituted in for y in either original equation to find the value of $x = 7$. The solution to the system is (7, 1) because it makes both equations true, and it is the point in which the

lines intersect. If the system is *dependent*—having infinitely many solutions—then both variables will cancel out when the elimination method is used, resulting in an equation that is true for many values of *x* and *y*. Since the system is dependent, both equations can be simplified to the same equation or line.

A system can also be solved using *substitution*. This involves solving one equation for a variable and then plugging that solved equation into the other equation in the system. This equation can be solved for one variable, which can then be plugged in to either original equation and solved for the other variable. For example, $x - y = -2$ and $3x + 2y = 9$ can be solved using substitution. The first equation can be solved for x, where $x = -2 + y$. Then it can be plugged into the other equation:

$$3(-2 + y) + 2y = 9$$

Solving for y yields:

$$-6 + 3y + 2y = 9$$

That shows that $y = 3$. If $y = 3$, then $x = 1$.

This solution can be checked by plugging in these values for the variables in each equation to see if it makes a true statement.

Finally, a solution to a system of equations can be found graphically. The solution to a linear system is the point or points where the lines cross. The values of x and y represent the coordinates (x, y) where the lines intersect. Using the same system of equation as above, they can be solved for y to put them in slope-intercept form, $y = mx + b$. These equations become $y = x + 2$ and $y = -\frac{3}{2}x + 4.5$. The slope is the coefficient of x, and the y-intercept is the constant value.

This system with the solution is shown below:

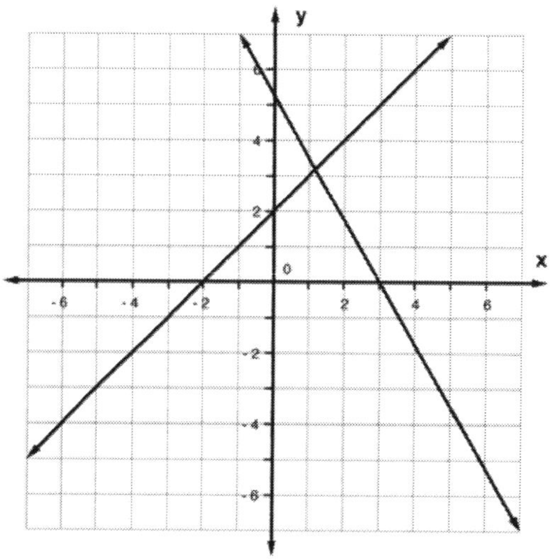

A system of equations may also be made up of a linear and a quadratic equation. These systems may have one solution, two solutions, or no solutions. The graph of these systems involves one straight line and one parabola. Algebraically, these systems can be solved by solving the linear equation for one variable and plugging that answer in to the quadratic equation. If possible, the equation can then be solved to find part of the answer. The graphing method is commonly used for these types of systems. On a graph, these two lines can be found to intersect at one point, at two points across the parabola, or at no points.

Linear Applications and Graphs

Graphing Functions and Relations

To graph relations and functions, the Cartesian plane is used. This means to think of the plane as being given a grid of squares, with one direction being the *x*-axis and the other direction the *y*-axis. Generally, the independent variable is placed along the horizontal axis, and the dependent variable is placed along the vertical axis. Any point on the plane can be specified by saying how far to go along the *x*-axis and how far along the *y*-axis with a pair of numbers (x, y). Specific values for these pairs can be given names such as $C = (-1, 3)$. Negative values mean to move left or down; positive values mean to move right or up. The point where the axes cross one another is called the *origin*. The origin has coordinates $(0, 0)$ and is usually called *O* when given a specific label.

An illustration of the Cartesian plane, along with graphs of $(2, 1)$ and $(-1, -1)$, are below:

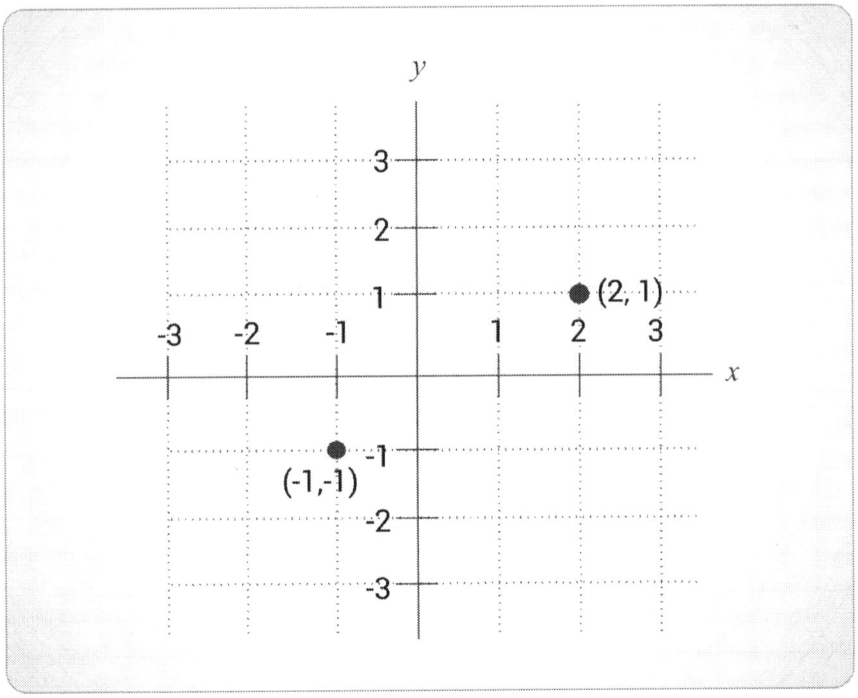

Relations also can be graphed by marking each point whose coordinates satisfy the relation. If the relation is a function, then there is only one value of y for any given value of x. This leads to the **vertical line test**: if a relation is graphed, then the relation is a function if any possible vertical line drawn anywhere along the graph would only touch the graph of the relation in no more than one place. Conversely, when graphing a function, then any possible vertical line drawn will not touch the graph of the function at any point or will touch the function at just one point. This test is made from the definition of a function, where each x-value must be mapped to one and only one y-value.

Rate of Change

The rate of change for a linear function is constant and can be determined based on a few representations. One method is to place the equation in slope-intercept form: $y = mx + b$. Thus, m is the slope, and b is the y-intercept. In the graph below, the equation is $y = x + 1$, where the slope is 1 and the y-intercept is 1. For every vertical change of 1 unit, there is a horizontal change of 1 unit.

The x-intercept is -1, which is the point where the line crosses the x-axis:

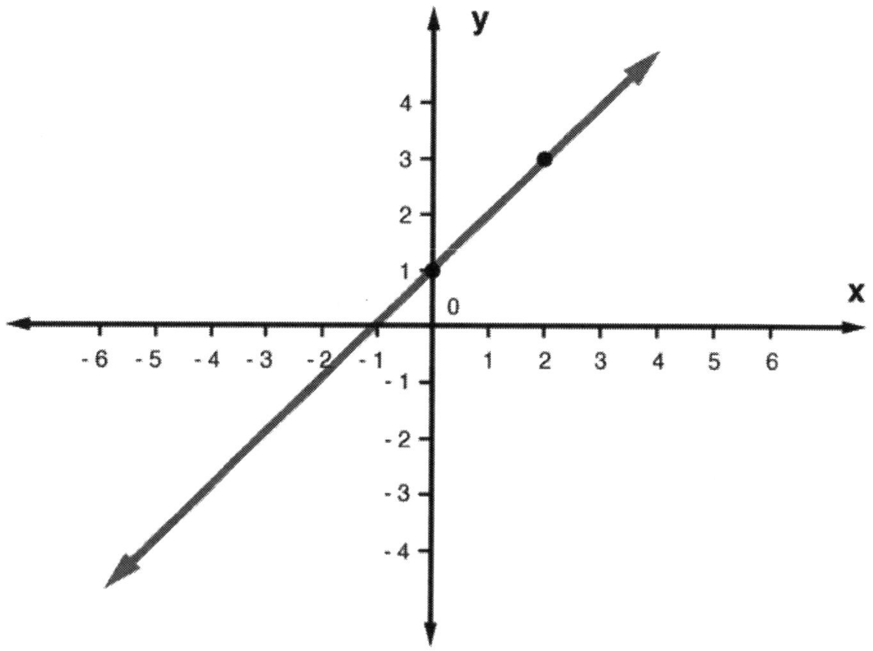

Probability Sets

Given a set of possible outcomes *X*, a *probability distribution* on *X* is a function that assigns a probability to each possible outcome. If the outcomes are $(x_1, x_2, x_3, \ldots x_n)$, and the probability distribution is *p*, then the following rules are applied.

- $0 \leq p(x_i) \leq 1$, for any i.
- $\sum_{i=1}^{n} p(x_i) = 1$.

In other words, the probability of a given outcome must be between zero and 1, while the total probability must be 1.

If $p(x_i)$ is constant, then this is called a *uniform probability distribution*, and $p(x_i) = \frac{1}{n}$. For example, on a six-sided die, the probability of each of the six outcomes will be $\frac{1}{6}$.

If seeking the probability of an outcome occurring in some specific range *A* of possible outcomes, written $P(A)$, add up the probabilities for each outcome in that range. For example, consider a six-sided die, and figure the probability of getting a 3 or lower when it is rolled. The possible rolls are 1, 2, 3, 4, 5, and 6. So, to get a 3 or lower, a roll of 1, 2, or 3 must be completed. The probabilities of each of these is $\frac{1}{6}$, so add these to get:

$$p(1) + p(2) + p(3) = \frac{1}{6} + \frac{1}{6} + \frac{1}{6} = \frac{1}{2}$$

Conditional Probabilities

An outcome occasionally lies within some range of possibilities *B*, and the probability that the outcomes also lie within some set of possibilities *A* needs to be figured. This is called a *conditional probability*. It is written as $P(A|B)$, which is read "the probability of *A* given *B*." The general formula for computing conditional probabilities is:

$$P(A|B) = \frac{P(A \cap B)}{P(B)}$$

However, when dealing with uniform probability distributions, simplify this a bit. Write $|A|$ to indicate the number of outcomes in *A*. Then, for uniform probability distributions, write:

$$P(A|B) = \frac{|A \cap B|}{|B|}$$

Recall that $A \cap B$ means "*A* intersect *B*," and consists of all of the outcomes that lie in both *A* and *B*.

This means that all possible outcomes do not need to be known. To see why this formula works, suppose that the set of outcomes *X* is $(x_1, x_2, x_3, \dots x_n)$, so that $|X| = n$. Then, for a uniform probability distribution:

$$P(A) = \frac{|A|}{n}$$

However, this means:

$$(A|B) = \frac{P(A \cap B)}{P(B)} = \frac{\frac{|A \cap B|}{n}}{\frac{|B|}{n}} = \frac{|A \cap B|}{|B|}$$

(since the *n*'s cancel out)

For example, suppose a die is rolled and it is known that it will land between 1 and 4. However, how many sides the die has is unknown. Figure the probability that the die is rolled higher than 2. To figure this, $P(3)$ or $P(4)$ does not need to be determined, or any of the other probabilities, since it is known that a fair die has a uniform probability distribution. Therefore, apply the formula $\frac{|A \cap B|}{|B|}$. So, in this case *B* is (1, 2, 3, 4) and $A \cap B$ is (3, 4). Therefore:

$$\frac{|A \cap B|}{|B|} = \frac{2}{4} = \frac{1}{2}$$

Conditional probability is an important concept because, in many situations, the likelihood of one outcome can differ radically depending on how something else comes out. The probability of passing a test given that one has studied all of the material is generally much higher than the probability of passing a test given that one has not studied at all. The probability of a person having heart trouble is much lower if that person exercises regularly. The probability that a college student will graduate is higher when his or her SAT scores are higher, and so on. For this reason, there are many people who are interested in conditional probabilities.

Note that in some practical situations, changing the order of the conditional probabilities can make the outcome very different. For example, the probability that a person with heart trouble has exercised regularly is quite different than the probability that a person who exercises regularly will have heart trouble. The probability of a person receiving a military-only award, given that he or she is or was a soldier, is generally not very high, but the probability that a person being or having been a soldier, given that he or she received a military-only award, is 1.

However, in some cases, the outcomes do not influence one another this way. If the probability of *A* is the same regardless of whether *B* is given; that is, if $P(A|B) = P(A)$, then *A* and *B* are considered *independent*. In this case:

$$P(A|B) = \frac{P(A \cap B)}{P(B)} = P(A)$$

$$P(A \cap B) = P(A)P(B)$$

In fact, if $P(A \cap B) = P(A)P(B)$, it can be determined that $P(A|B) = P(A)$ and $P(A|B) = P(B)$ by working backward. Therefore, *B* is also independent of *A*.

An example of something being independent can be seen in rolling dice. In this case, consider a red die and a green die. It is expected that when the dice are rolled, the outcome of the green die should not depend in any way on the outcome of the red die. Or, to take another example, if the same die is rolled repeatedly, then the next number rolled should not depend on which numbers have been rolled previously. Similarly, if a coin is flipped, then the next flip's outcome does not depend on the outcomes of previous flips.

This can sometimes be counter-intuitive, since when rolling a die or flipping a coin, there can be a streak of surprising results. If, however, it is known that the die or coin is fair, then these results are just the result of the fact that over long periods of time, it is very likely that some unlikely streaks of outcomes will occur. Therefore, avoid making the mistake of thinking that when considering a series of independent outcomes, a particular outcome is "due to happen" simply because a surprising series of outcomes has already been seen.

There is a second type of common mistake that people tend to make when reasoning about statistical outcomes: the idea that when something of low probability happens, this is surprising. It would be surprising that something with low probability happened after just one attempt. However, with so much happening all at once, it is easy to see at least something happen in a way that seems to have a very low probability. In fact, a lottery is a good example. The odds of winning a lottery are very small, but the odds that somebody wins the lottery each week are actually fairly high. Therefore, no one should be surprised when some low probability things happen.

Addition Rule

The *addition rule* for probabilities states that the probability of *A* or *B* happening is $P(A \cup B) = P(A) + P(B) - P(A \cap B)$. Note that the subtraction of $P(A \cap B)$ must be performed, or else it would result in double counting any outcomes that lie in both *A* and in *B*. For example, suppose that a 20-sided die is being rolled. Fred bets that the outcome will be greater than 10, while Helen bets that it will be greater than 4 but less than 15. What is the probability that at least one of them is correct?

We apply the rule:

$$P(A \cup B) = P(A) + P(B) - P(A \cap B)$$

A is that outcome *x* is in the range $x > 10$, and *B* is that outcome *x* is in the range $4 < x < 15$.

$P(A) = 10 \times \frac{1}{20} = \frac{1}{2}$. $P(B) = 10 \times \frac{1}{20} = \frac{1}{2}$. $P(A \cap B)$ can be computed by noting that $A \cap B$ means the outcome *x* is in the range $10 < x < 15$, so $P(A \cap B) = 4 \times \frac{1}{20} = \frac{1}{5}$.

Therefore:

$$P(A \cup B) = P(A) + P(B) - P(A \cap B) = \frac{1}{2} + \frac{1}{2} - \frac{1}{5} = \frac{4}{5}$$

Note that in this particular example, we could also have directly reasoned about the set of possible outcomes $A \cup B$, by noting that this would mean that *x* must be in the range $5 \leq x$. However, this is not always the case, depending on the given information.

Multiplication Rule

The *multiplication rule* for probabilities states the probability of *A* and *B* both happening is:

$$P(A \cap B) = P(A)P(B|A)$$

As an example, suppose that when Jamie wears black pants, there is a ½ probability that she wears a black shirt as well, and that she wears black pants ¾ of the time. What is the probability that she is wearing both a black shirt and black pants?

To figure this, use the above formula, where *A* will be "Jamie is wearing black pants," while *B* will be "Jamie is wearing a black shirt." It is known that $P(A)$ is ¾. It is also known that $P(B|A) = \frac{1}{2}$. Multiplying the two, the probability that she is wearing both black pants and a black shirt is:

$$P(A)P(B|A) = \frac{3}{4} \times \frac{1}{2} = \frac{3}{8}$$

Descriptive Statistics

What are Statistics?

The field of statistics describes relationships between quantities that are related, but not necessarily in a deterministic manner. For example, a graduating student's salary will often be higher when the student graduates with a higher GPA, but this is not always the case. Likewise, people who smoke tobacco are more likely to develop lung cancer, but, in fact, it is possible for non-smokers to develop the disease as well. *Statistics* describes these kinds of situations, where the likelihood of some outcome depends on the starting data.

Descriptive statistics involves analyzing a collection of data to describe its broad properties such average (or mean), what percent of the data falls within a given range, and other such properties. An example of this would be taking all of the test scores from a given class and calculating the average test score. *Inferential statistics* attempts to use data about a subset of some population to make inferences about the rest of the population. An example of this would be taking a collection of students who received tutoring and comparing their results to a collection of students who did not receive tutoring, then using that comparison to try to predict whether the tutoring program in question is beneficial.

To be sure that inferences have a high probability of being true for the whole population, the subset that is analyzed needs to resemble a miniature version of the population as closely as possible. For this reason, statisticians like to choose random samples from the population to study, rather than picking a specific group of people based on some similarity. For example, studying the incomes of people who live in Portland does not tell anything useful about the incomes of people who live in Tallahassee.

Mean, Median, and Mode

Suppose that *X* is a set of data points $(x_1, x_2, x_3, \dots x_n)$ and some description of the general properties of this data need to be found.

The first property that can be defined for this set of data is the *mean*. To find the mean, add up all the data points, then divide by the total number of data points. This can be expressed using *summation notation* as:

$$\bar{X} = \frac{x_1 + x_2 + x_3 + \cdots + x_n}{n} = \frac{1}{n}\sum_{i=1}^{n} x_i$$

For example, suppose that in a class of 10 students, the scores on a test were 50, 60, 65, 65, 75, 80, 85, 85, 90, 100. Therefore, the average test score will be:

$$\frac{1}{10}(50 + 60 + 65 + 65 + 75 + 80 + 85 + 85 + 90 + 100) = 75.5$$

The mean is a useful number if the distribution of data is normal (more on this later), which roughly means that the frequency of different outcomes has a single peak and is roughly equally distributed on both sides of that peak. However, it is less useful in some cases where the data might be split or where there are some *outliers*. Outliers are data points that are far from the rest of the data. For example, suppose there are 90 employees and 10 executives at a company. The executives make $1000 per hour, and the employees make $10 per hour. Therefore, the average pay rate will be $\frac{1000 \times 10 + 10 \times 90}{100} = 109$, or $109 per hour. In this case, this average is not very descriptive.

Another useful measurement is the *median*. In a data set *X* consisting of data points $x_1, x_2, x_3, \dots x_n$, the median is the point in the middle. The middle refers to the point where half the data comes before it and half comes after, when the data is recorded in numerical order. If *n* is odd, then the median is $x_{\frac{n+1}{2}}$. If *n* is even, it is defined as $\frac{1}{2}\left(x_{\frac{n}{2}} + x_{\frac{n}{2}+1}\right)$, the mean of the two data points closest to the middle of the data points. In the previous example of test scores, the two middle points are 75 and 80. Since there is no single point, the average of these two scores needs to be found. The average is $\frac{75+80}{2} = 77.5$. The median is generally a good value to use if there are a few outliers in the data. It prevents those outliers from affecting the "middle" value as much as when using the mean.

Since an outlier is a data point that is far from most of the other data points in a data set, this means an outlier also is any point that is far from the median of the data set. The outliers can have a substantial effect on the mean of a data set, but usually do not change the median or mode, or do not change them by a large quantity. For example, consider the data set (3, 5, 6, 6, 6, 8). This has a median of 6 and a mode of 6, with a mean of $\frac{34}{6} \approx 5.67$. Now, suppose a new data point of 1000 is added so that the data set is now (3, 5, 6, 6, 6, 8, 1000). This does not change the median or mode, which are both still 6. However, the average is now $\frac{1034}{7}$, which is approximately 147.7. In this case, the median and mode will be better descriptions for most of the data points.

The reason for outliers in a given data set is a complicated problem. It is sometimes the result of an error by the experimenter, but often they are perfectly valid data points that must be taken into consideration.

One additional measure to define for X is the *mode*. This is the data point that appears more frequently. If two or more data points all tie for the most frequent appearance, then each of them is considered a mode. In the case of the test scores, where the numbers were 50, 60, 65, 65, 75, 80, 85, 85, 90, 100, there are two modes: 65 and 85.

Geometry Concepts

Plane Geometry

Locations on the plane that have no width or breadth are called *points*. These points usually will be denoted with capital letters such as P.

Any pair of points A, B on the plane will determine a unique straight line between them. This line is denoted AB. Sometimes to emphasize a line is being considered, this will be written as $\overleftrightarrow{AB}$.

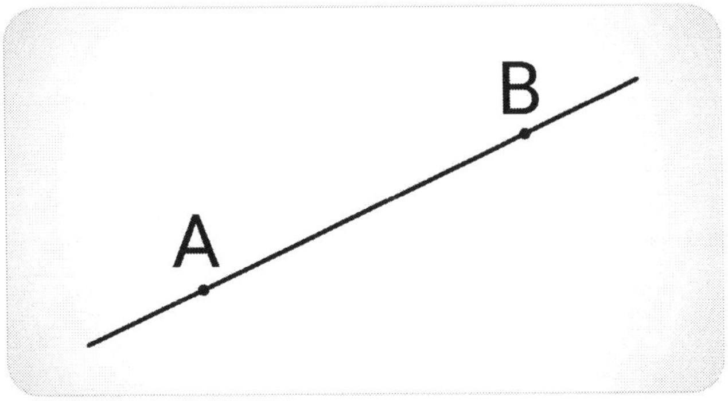

If the Cartesian coordinates for A and B are known, then the distance $d(A, B)$ along the line between them can be measured using the *Pythagorean formula*, which states that if:

$$A = (x_1, y_1) \text{ and } B = (x_2, y_2)$$

Then the distance between them is:

$$d(A, B) = \sqrt{(x_2 - x_1)^2 + (y_2 - y_1)^2}$$

The part of a line that lies between A and B is called a *line segment*. It has two endpoints, one at A and one at B. *Rays* also can be formed. Given points A and B, a *ray* is the portion of a line that starts at one of these points, passes through the other, and keeps on going. Therefore, a ray has a single endpoint, but the other end goes off to infinity.

Given a pair of points *A* and *B*, a circle centered at *A* and passing through *B* can be formed. This is the set of points whose distance from *A* is exactly $d(A, B)$. The radius of this circle will be $d(A, B)$.

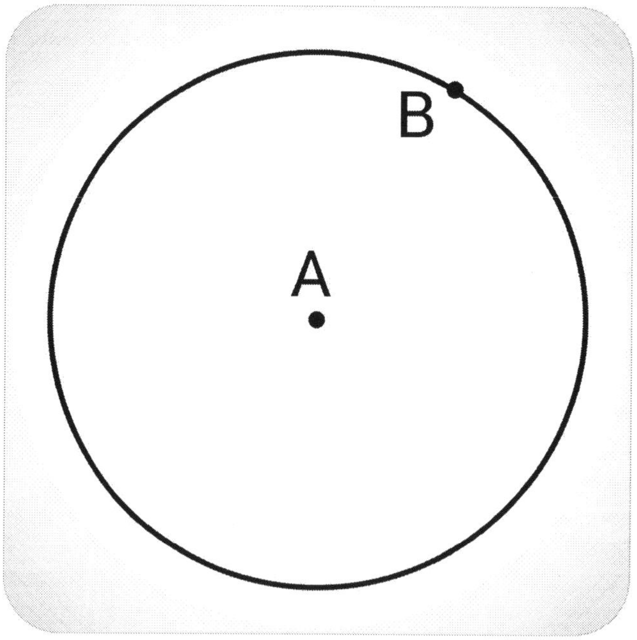

The *circumference* of a circle is the distance traveled by following the edge of the circle for one complete revolution, and the length of the circumference is given by $2\pi r$, where *r* is the radius of the circle. The formula for circumference is $C = 2\pi r$.

When two lines cross, they form an *angle*. The point where the lines cross is called the *vertex* of the angle. The angle can be named by either just using the vertex, $\angle A$, or else by listing three points $\angle BAC$, as shown in the diagram below.

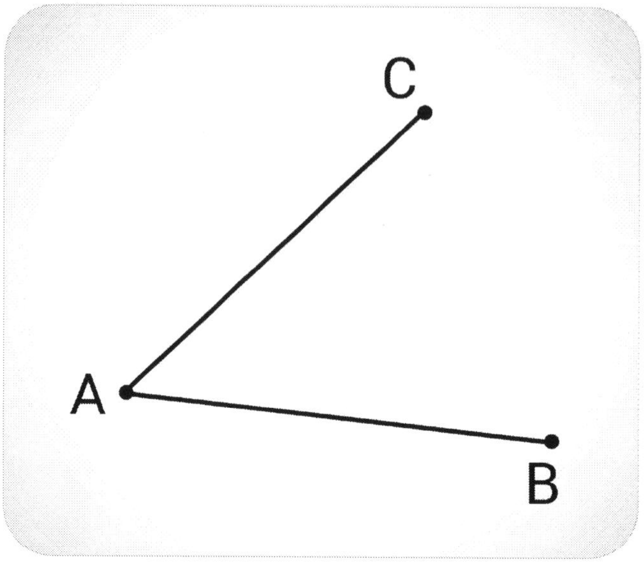

The measurement of an angle can be given in degrees or in radians. In degrees, a full circle is 360 degrees, written 360°. In radians, a full circle is 2π radians.

Given two points on the circumference of a circle, the path along the circle between those points is called an *arc* of the circle. For example, the arc between *B* and *C* is denoted by a thinner line:

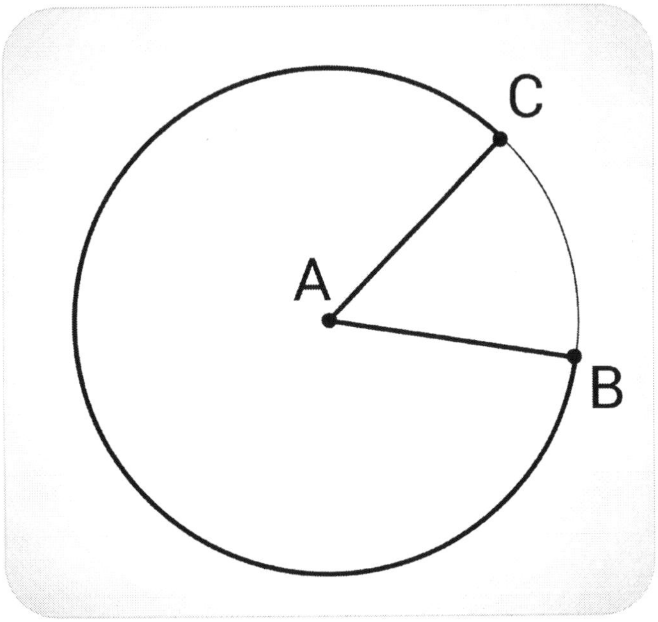

The length of the path along an arc is called the *arc length*. If the circle has radius *r*, then the arc length is given by multiplying the measure of the angle in radians by the radius of the circle.

Two lines are said to be *parallel* if they never intersect. If the lines are *AB* and *CD*, then this is written as $AB \parallel CD$.

If two lines cross to form four quarter-circles, that is, 90° angles, the two lines are *perpendicular*. If the point at which they cross is *B*, and the two lines are *AB* and *BC*, then this is written as $AB \perp BC$.

A *polygon* is a closed figure (meaning it divides the plane into an inside and an outside) consisting of a collection of line segments between points. These points are called the *vertices* of the polygon. These line segments must not overlap one another. Note that the number of sides is equal to the number of angles, or vertices of the polygon. The angles between line segments meeting one another in the polygon are called *interior angles*.

A *regular polygon* is a polygon whose edges are all the same length and whose interior angles are all of equal measure.

A *triangle* is a polygon with three sides. A *quadrilateral* is a polygon with four sides.

A *right triangle* is a triangle that has one 90° angle.

The sum of the interior angles of any triangle must add up to 180°.

An *isosceles triangle* is a triangle in which two of the sides are the same length. In this case, it will always have two congruent interior angles. If a triangle has two congruent interior angles, it will always be isosceles.

An *equilateral triangle* is a triangle whose sides are all the same length and whose angles are all equivalent to one another, equal to 60°. Equilateral triangles are examples of regular polygons. Note that equilateral triangles are also isosceles.

A *rectangle* is a quadrilateral whose interior angles are all 90°. A rectangle has two sets of sides that are equal to one another.

A *square* is a rectangle whose width and height are equal. Therefore, squares are regular polygons.

A *parallelogram* is a quadrilateral in which the opposite sides are parallel and equivalent to each other.

Transformations of a Plane

Given a figure drawn on a plane, many changes can be made to that figure, including *rotation*, *translation*, and *reflection*. Rotations turn the figure about a point, translations slide the figure, and reflections flip the figure over a specified line. When performing these transformations, the original figure is called the *pre-image*, and the figure after transformation is called the *image*.

More specifically, *translation* means that all points in the figure are moved in the same direction by the same distance. In other words, the figure is slid in some fixed direction. Of course, while the entire figure is slid by the same distance, this does not change any of the measurements of the figures involved. The result will have the same distances and angles as the original figure.

In terms of Cartesian coordinates, a translation means a shift of each of the original points (x, y) by a fixed amount in the *x* and *y* directions, to become $(x + a, y + b)$.

Another procedure that can be performed is called *reflection*. To do this, a line in the plane is specified, called the *line of reflection*. Then, take each point and flip it over the line so that it is the same distance from the line but on the opposite side of it. This does not change any of the distances or angles involved, but it does reverse the order in which everything appears.

To reflect something over the *x*-axis, the points (x, y) are sent to $(x, -y)$. To reflect something over the *y*-axis, the points (x, y) are sent to the points $(-x, y)$. Flipping over other lines is not something easy to express in Cartesian coordinates. However, by drawing the figure and the line of reflection, the distance to the line and the original points can be used to find the reflected figure.

Example: Reflect this triangle with vertices (-1, 0), (2, 1), and (2, 0) over the *y*-axis. The pre-image is shown below.

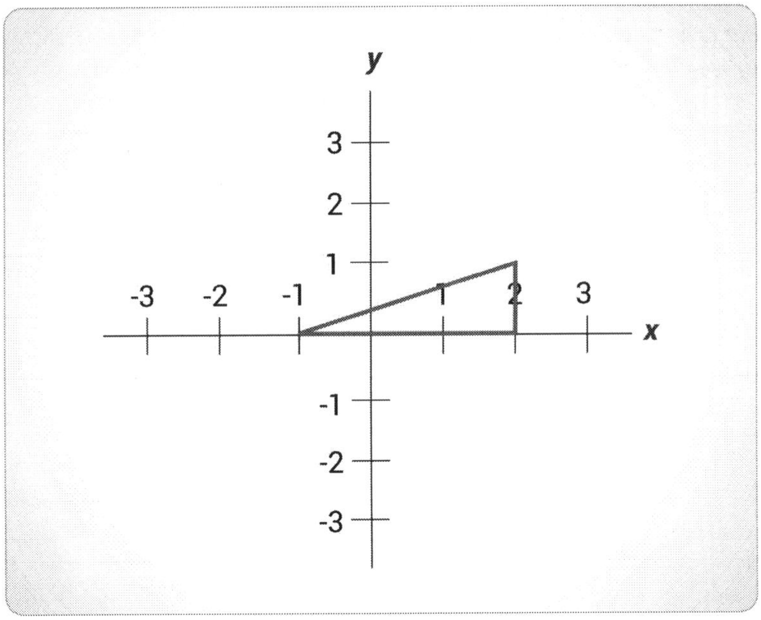

To do this, flip the *x* values of the points involved to the negatives of themselves, while keeping the *y* values the same. The image is shown here.

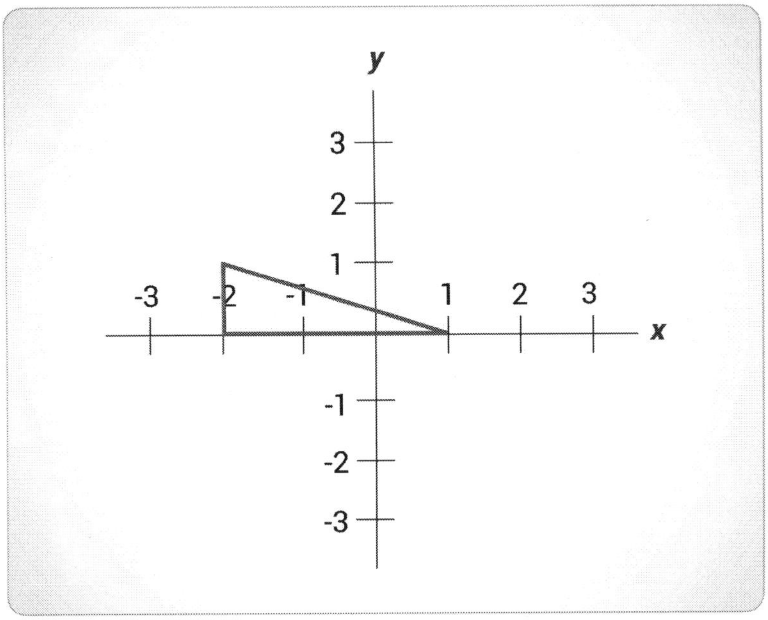

The new vertices will be (1, 0), (-2, 1), and (-2, 0).

Another procedure that does not change the distances and angles in a figure is *rotation*. In this procedure, pick a center point, then rotate every vertex along a circle around that point by the same angle. This procedure is also not easy to express in Cartesian coordinates, and this is not a requirement on this test. However, as with reflections, it's helpful to draw the figures and see what the result of the rotation would look like. This transformation can be performed using a compass and protractor.

Each one of these transformations can be performed on the coordinate plane without changes to the original dimensions or angles.

If two figures in the plane involve the same distances and angles, they are called *congruent figures*. In other words, two figures are congruent when they go from one form to another through reflection, rotation, and translation, or a combination of these.

Remember that rotation and translation will give back a new figure that is identical to the original figure, but reflection will give back a mirror image of it.

To recognize that a figure has undergone a rotation, check to see that the figure has not been changed into a mirror image, but that its orientation has changed (that is, whether the parts of the figure now form different angles with the *x* and *y* axes).

To recognize that a figure has undergone a translation, check to see that the figure has not been changed into a mirror image, and that the orientation remains the same.

To recognize that a figure has undergone a reflection, check to see that the new figure is a mirror image of the old figure.

Keep in mind that sometimes a combination of translations, reflections, and rotations may be performed on a figure.

Dilation

A *dilation* is a transformation that preserves angles, but not distances. This can be thought of as stretching or shrinking a figure. If a dilation makes figures larger, it is called an *enlargement*. If a dilation makes figures smaller, it is called a *reduction*. The easiest example is to dilate around the origin. In this case, multiply the *x* and *y* coordinates by a *scale factor*, k, sending points (x, y) to (kx, ky).

As an example, draw a dilation of the following triangle, whose vertices will be the points (-1, 0), (1, 0), and (1, 1).

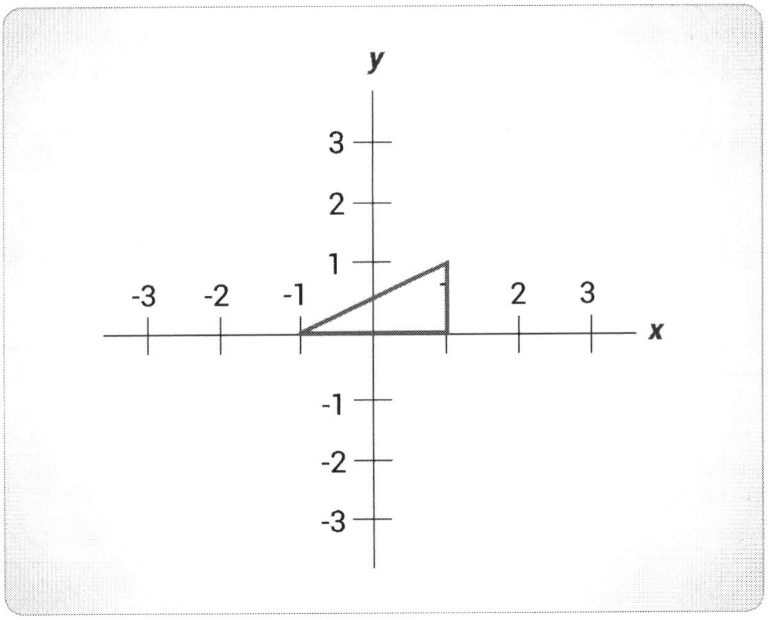

For this problem, dilate by a scale factor of 2, so the new vertices will be (-2, 0), (2, 0), and (2, 2).

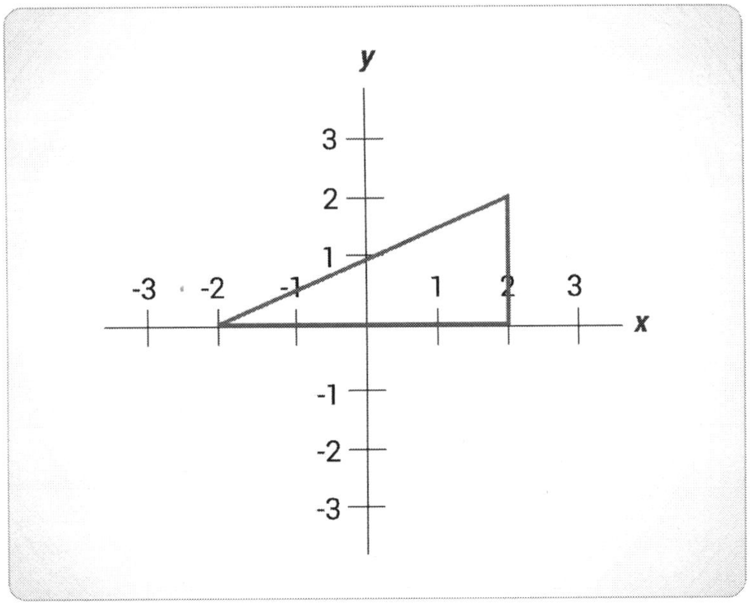

Note that after a dilation, the distances between the vertices of the figure will have changed, but the angles remain the same. The two figures that are obtained by dilation, along with possibly translation, rotation, and reflection, are all *similar* to one another. Another way to think of this is that similar figures have the same number of vertices and edges, and their angles are all the same. Similar figures have the same basic shape, but are different in size.

Symmetry

Using the types of transformations above, if an object can undergo these changes and not appear to have changed, then the figure is symmetrical. If an object can be split in half by a line and flipped over that line to lie directly on top of itself, it is said to have *line symmetry*. An example of both types of figures is seen below.

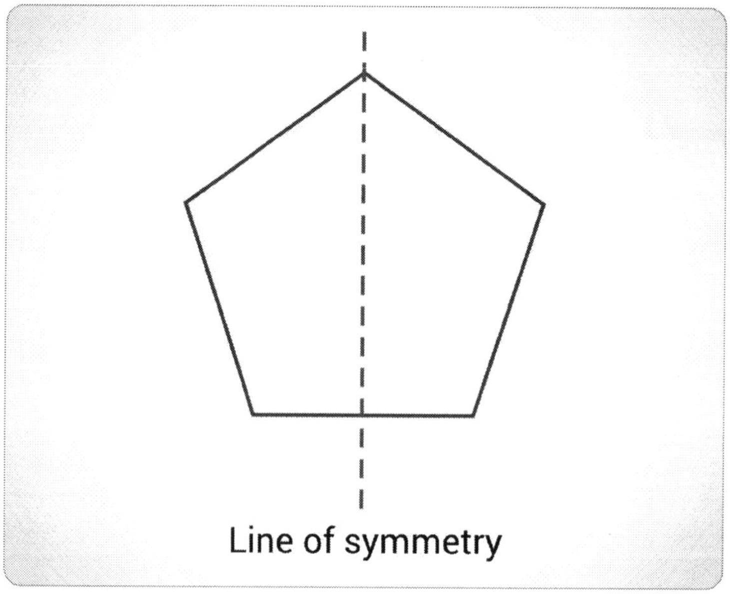

If an object can be rotated about its center to any degree smaller than 360, and it lies directly on top of itself, the object is said to have *rotational symmetry*. An example of this type of symmetry is shown below. The pentagon has an order of 5.

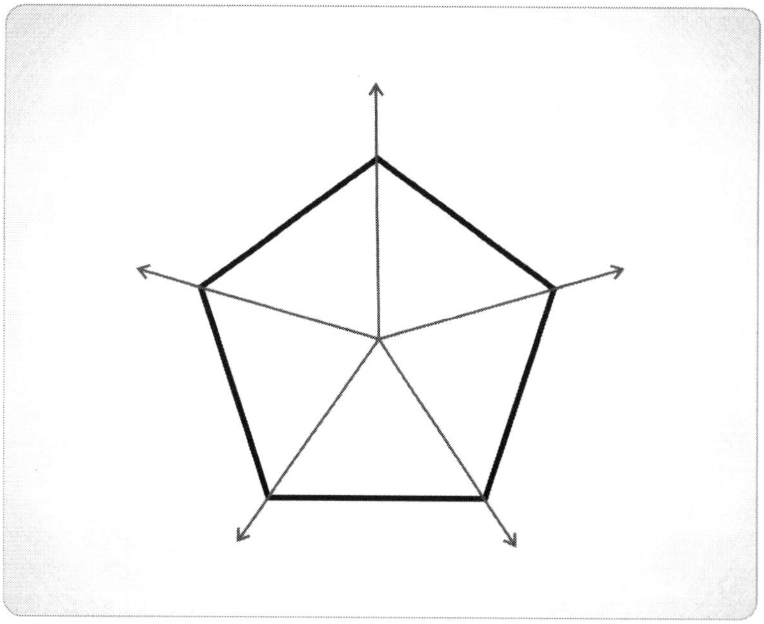

The rotational symmetry lines in the figure above can be used to find the angles formed at the center of the pentagon. Knowing that all of the angles together form a full circle, at 360 degrees, the figure can be split into 5 angles equally. By dividing the 360° by 5, each angle is 72°.

Given the length of one side of the figure, the perimeter of the pentagon can also be found using rotational symmetry. If one side length was 3 cm, that side length can be rotated onto each other side length four times. This would give a total of 5 side lengths equal to 3 cm. To find the perimeter, or distance around the figure, multiply 3 by 5. The perimeter of the figure would be 15 cm.

If a line cannot be drawn anywhere on the object to flip the figure onto itself or rotated less than or equal to 180 degrees to lay on top of itself, the object is asymmetrical. Examples of these types of figures are shown below.

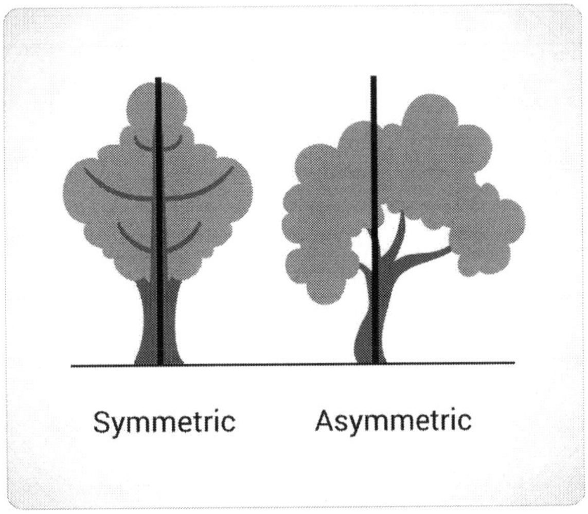

Perimeter and Area

Perimeter is the measurement of a distance around something or the sum of all sides of a polygon. Think of perimeter as the length of the boundary, like a fence. In contrast, *area* is the space occupied by a defined enclosure, like a field enclosed by a fence.

When thinking about perimeter, think about walking around the outside of something. When thinking about area, think about the amount of space or *surface area* something takes up.

Square
The perimeter of a square is measured by adding together all of the sides. Since a square has four equal sides, its perimeter can be calculated by multiplying the length of one side by 4. Thus, the formula is $P = 4 \times s$, where s equals one side. For example, the following square has side lengths of 5 meters:

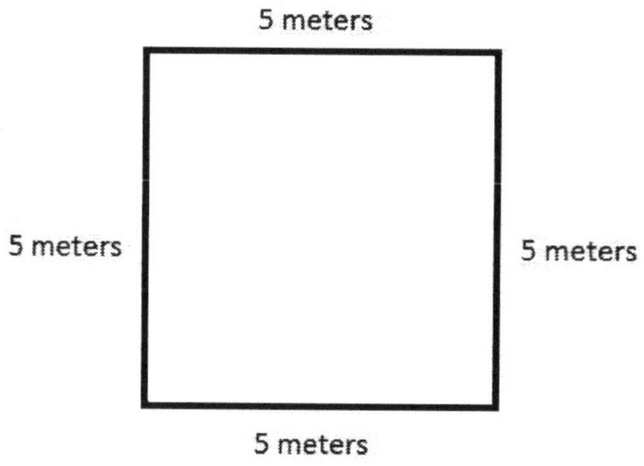

The perimeter is 20 meters because 4 times 5 is 20.

The area of a square is the length of a side squared, and the area of a rectangle is length multiplied by the width. For example, if the length of the square is 7 centimeters, then the area is 49 square centimeters. The formula for this example is $A = s^2 = 7^2 = 49$ square centimeters. An example is if the rectangle has a length of 6 inches and a width of 7 inches, then the area is 42 square inches:

$$A = lw = 6(7) = 42 \text{ square inches}$$

Rectangle
Like a square, a rectangle's perimeter is measured by adding together all of the sides. But as the sides are unequal, the formula is different. A rectangle has equal values for its lengths (long sides) and equal values for its widths (short sides), so the perimeter formula for a rectangle is:

$$P = l + l + w + w = 2l + 2w$$

l equals length
w equals width

The area is found by multiplying the length by the width, so the formula is $A = l \times w$.

For example, if the length of a rectangle is 10 inches and the width 8 inches, then the perimeter is 36 inches because:

$$P = 2l + 2w = 2(10) + 2(8) = 20 + 16 = 36 \text{ inches}$$

Triangle
A triangle's perimeter is measured by adding together the three sides, so the formula is $P = a + b + c$, where a, b, and c are the values of the three sides. The area is the product of one-half the base and height so the formula is:

$$A = \frac{1}{2} \times b \times h$$

It can be simplified to:

$$A = \frac{bh}{2}$$

The base is the bottom of the triangle, and the height is the distance from the base to the peak. If a problem asks to calculate the area of a triangle, it will provide the base and height.

For example, if the base of the triangle is 2 feet and the height 4 feet, then the area is 4 square feet. The following equation shows the formula used to calculate the area of the triangle:

$$\text{A} = \frac{1}{2}\text{bh} = \frac{1}{2}(2)(4) = 4 \text{ square feet}$$

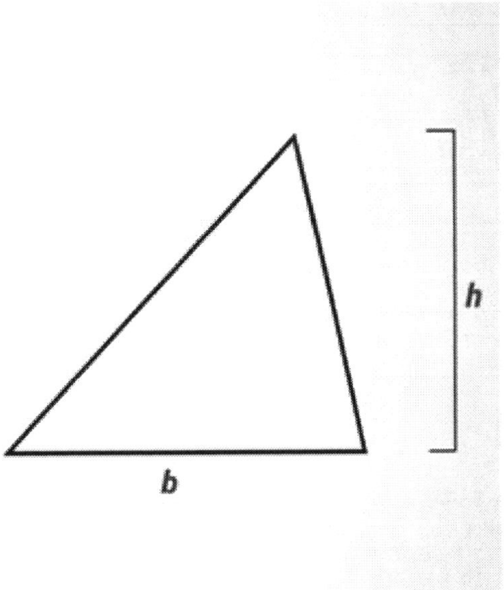

Circle
A circle's perimeter—also known as its circumference—is measured by multiplying the diameter by π.

Diameter is the straight line measured from one end to the direct opposite end of the circle.

π is referred to as pi and is equal to 3.14 (with rounding).

So the formula is $\pi \times d$.

This is sometimes expressed by the formula $C = 2 \times \pi \times r$, where r is the radius of the circle. These formulas are equivalent, as the radius equals half of the diameter.

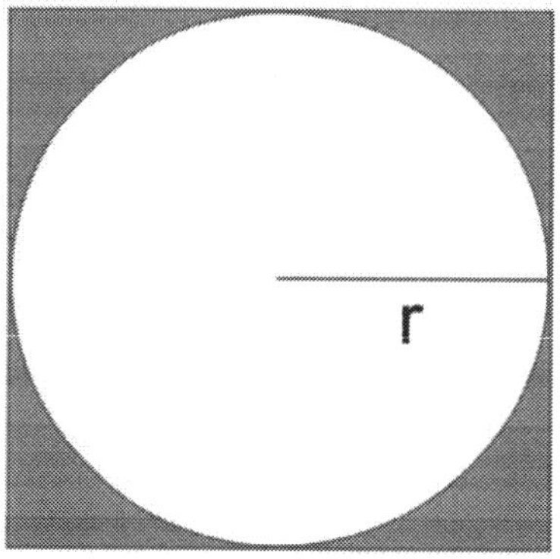

The area of a circle is calculated through the formula $A = \pi \times r^2$. The test will indicate either to leave the answer with π attached or to calculate to the nearest decimal place, which means multiplying by 3.14 for π.

To find the areas of more *general polygons*, it is usually easiest to break up the polygon into rectangles and triangles. For example, find the area of the following figure whose vertices are (-1, 0), (-1, 2), (1, 3), and (1, 0).

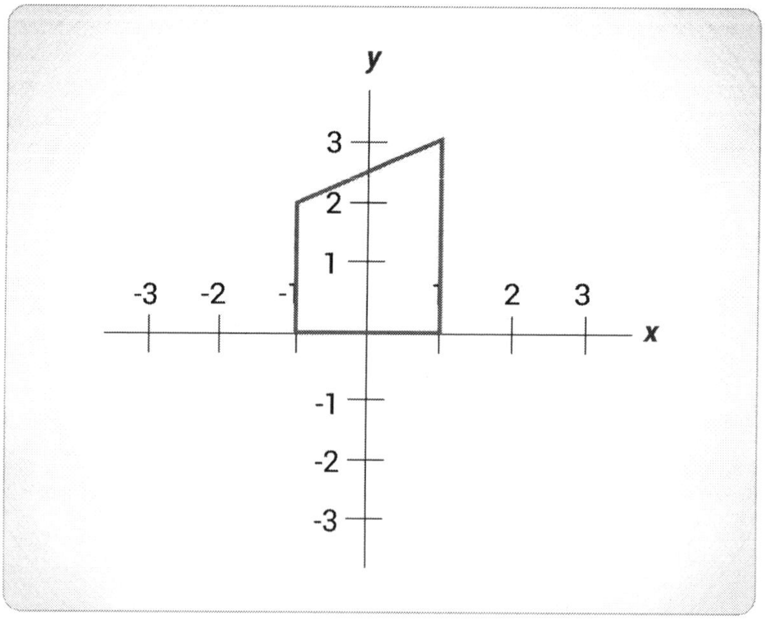

Separate this into a rectangle and a triangle as shown:

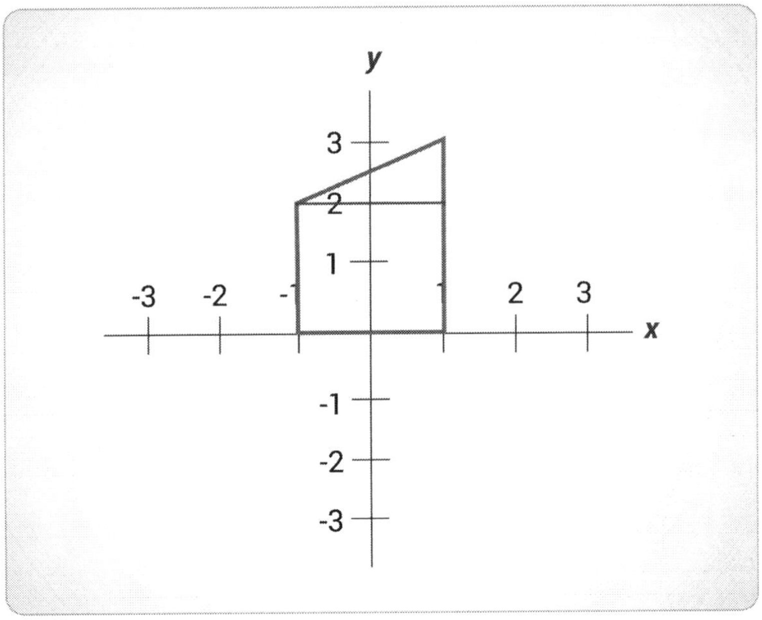

The rectangle has a height of 2 and a width of 2, so it has a total area of $2 \times 2 = 4$. The triangle has a width of 2 and a height of 1, so it has an area of $\frac{1}{2} 2 \times 1 = 1$. Therefore, the entire quadrilateral has an area of 4 + 1 = 5.

As another example, suppose someone wants to tile a rectangular room that is 10 feet by 6 feet using triangular tiles that are 12 inches by 6 inches. How many tiles would be needed? To figure this, first find the area of the room, which will be $10 \times 6 = 60$ square feet. The dimensions of the triangle are 1 foot by ½ foot, so the area of each triangle is $\frac{1}{2} \times 1 \times \frac{1}{2} = \frac{1}{4}$ square feet. Notice that the dimensions of the triangle had to be converted to the same units as the rectangle. Now, take the total area divided by the area of one tile to find the answer: $\frac{60}{\frac{1}{4}} = 60 \times 4 = 240$ tiles required.

Irregular Shapes

The perimeter of an irregular polygon is found by adding the lengths of all of the sides. In cases where all of the sides are given, this will be very straightforward, as it will simply involve finding the sum of the provided lengths. Other times, a side length may be missing and must be determined before the perimeter can be calculated. Consider the example below:

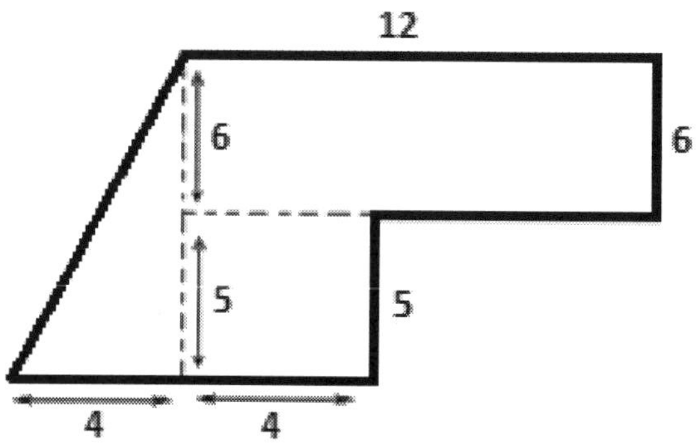

All of the side lengths are provided except for the angled side on the left. Test takers should notice that this is the hypotenuse of a right triangle. The other two sides of the triangle are provided (the base is 4 and the height is 6 + 5 = 11). The Pythagorean Theorem can be used to find the length of the hypotenuse, remembering that $a^2 + b^2 = c^2$.

Substituting the side values provided yields $(4)^2 + (11)^2 = c^2$.

Therefore, c = $\sqrt{16 + 121} = 11.7$

Finally, the perimeter can be found by adding this new side length with the other provided lengths to get the total length around the figure: 4+4+5+8+6+12+11.7=50.7. Although units are not provided in this figure, remember that reporting units with a measurement is important.

The area of an irregular polygon is found by decomposing, or breaking apart, the figure into smaller shapes. When the area of the smaller shapes is determined, these areas are added together to produce the total area of the area of the original figure. Consider the same example provided before:

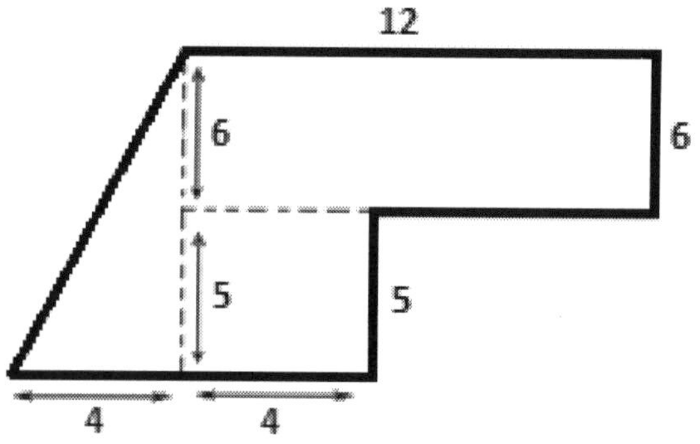

The irregular polygon is decomposed into two rectangles and a triangle. The area of the large rectangles ($A = l \times w \rightarrow A = 12 \times 6$) is 72 square units. The area of the small rectangle is 20 square units ($A = 4 \times 5$). The area of the triangle ($A = \frac{1}{2} \times b \times h \rightarrow A = \frac{1}{2} \times 4 \times 11$) is 22 square units. The sum of the areas of these figures produces the total area of the original polygon: $A = 72 + 20 + 22 \rightarrow A = 114$ square units.

Arc

The *arc of a circle* is the distance between two points on the circle. The length of the arc of a circle in terms of *degrees* is easily determined if the value of the central angle is known. The length of the arc is simply the value of the central angle. In this example, the length of the arc of the circle in degrees is 75°.

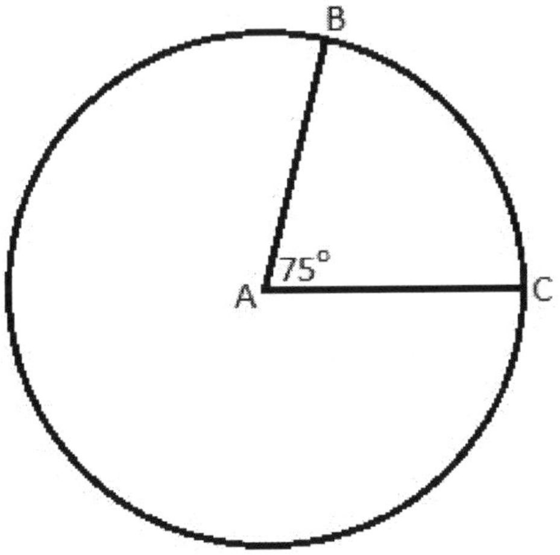

To determine the length of the arc of a circle in *distance*, the student will need to know the values for both the central angle and the radius. This formula is:

$$\frac{central\ angle}{360°} = \frac{arc\ length}{2\pi r}$$

The equation is simplified by cross-multiplying to solve for the arc length.

In the following example, the student should substitute the values of the central angle (75°) and the radius (10 inches) into the equation above to solve for the arc length.

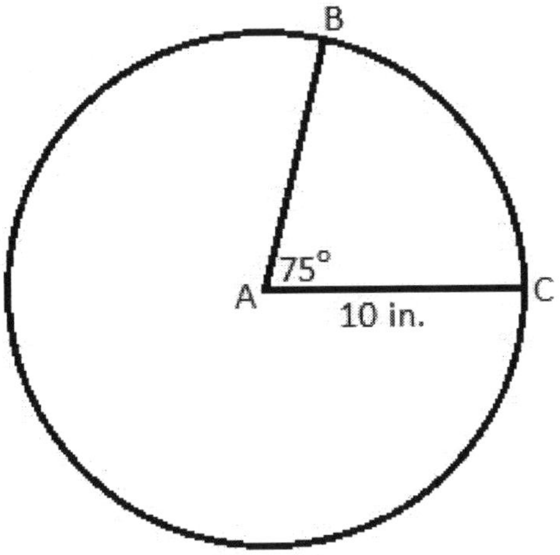

$$\frac{75°}{360°} = \frac{\text{arc length}}{2(3.14)(10\text{in.})}$$

To solve the equation, first cross-multiply: 4710 = 360(arc length). Next, divide each side of the equation by 360. The result of the formula is that the arc length is 13.1 (rounded).

Volumes and Surface Areas

Geometry in three dimensions is similar to geometry in two dimensions. The main new feature is that three points now define a unique *plane* that passes through each of them. Three dimensional objects can be made by putting together two dimensional figures in different surfaces. Below, some of the possible three dimensional figures will be provided, along with formulas for their volumes and surface areas.

A rectangular prism is a box whose sides are all rectangles meeting at 90° angles. Such a box has three dimensions: length, width, and height. If the length is *x*, the width is *y*, and the height is *z*, then the volume is given by $V = xyz$.

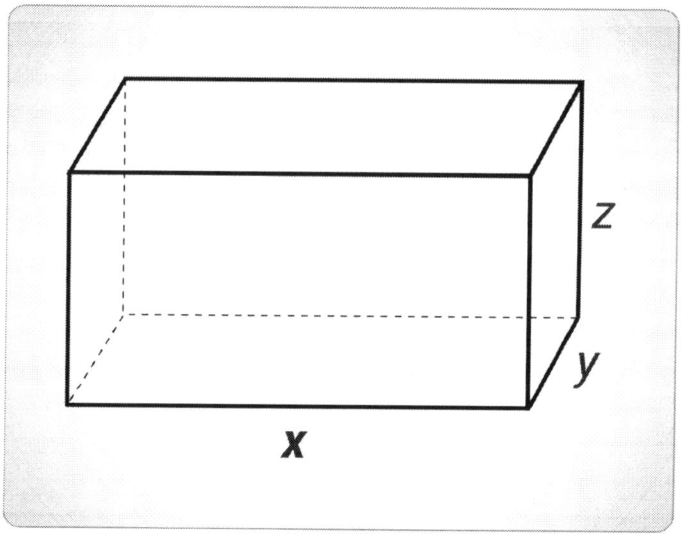

The surface area will be given by computing the surface area of each rectangle and adding them together. There are a total of six rectangles. Two of them have sides of length *x* and *y*, two have sides of length *y* and *z*, and two have sides of length *x* and *z*. Therefore, the total surface area will be given by $SA = 2xy + 2yz + 2xz$.

A *rectangular pyramid* is a figure with a rectangular base and four triangular sides that meet at a single vertex. If the rectangle has sides of length *x* and *y*, then the volume will be given by $V = \frac{1}{3}xyh$.

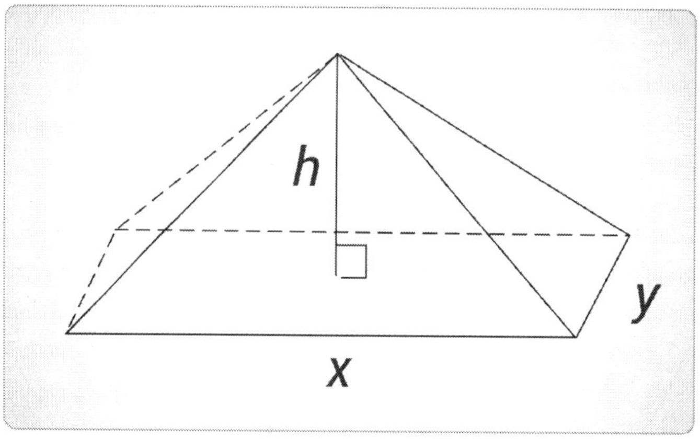

To find the surface area, the dimensions of each triangle need to be known. However, these dimensions can differ depending on the problem in question. Therefore, there is no general formula for calculating total surface area.

A *sphere* is a set of points all of which are equidistant from some central point. It is like a circle, but in three dimensions. The volume of a sphere of radius *r* is given by $V = \frac{4}{3}\pi r^3$. The surface area is given by $A = 4\pi r^2$.

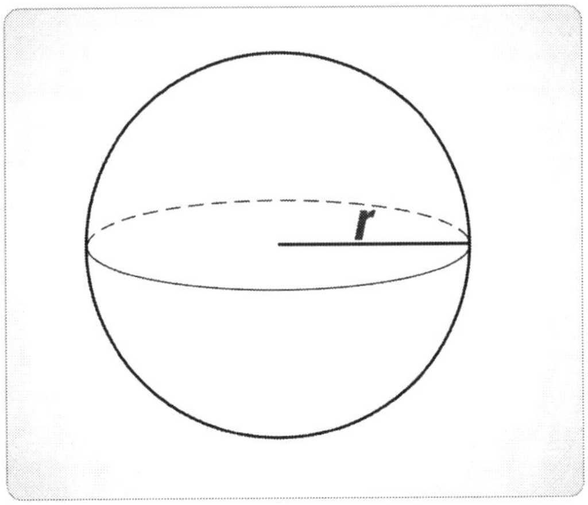

The Pythagorean Theorem

The Pythagorean theorem is an important result in geometry. It states that for right triangles, the sum of the squares of the two shorter sides will be equal to the square of the longest side (also called the *hypotenuse*). The longest side will always be the side opposite to the 90° angle. If this side is called *c*, and the other two sides are *a* and *b*, then the Pythagorean theorem states that $c^2 = a^2 + b^2$. Since lengths are always positive, this also can be written as $c = \sqrt{a^2 + b^2}$.

A diagram to show the parts of a triangle using the Pythagorean theorem is below.

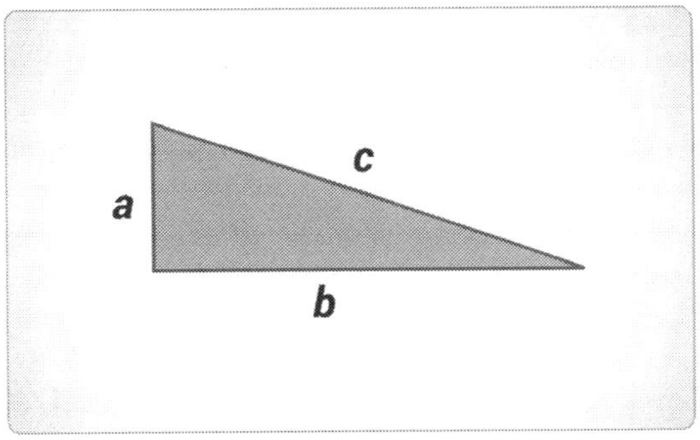

As an example of the theorem, suppose that Shirley has a rectangular field that is 5 feet wide and 12 feet long, and she wants to split it in half using a fence that goes from one corner to the opposite corner. How long will this fence need to be? To figure this out, note that this makes the field into two right triangles, whose hypotenuse will be the fence dividing it in half. Therefore, the fence length will be given by $\sqrt{5^2 + 12^2} = \sqrt{169} = 13$ feet long.

Similar Figures and Proportions

Sometimes, two figures are similar, meaning they have the same basic shape and the same interior angles, but they have different dimensions. If the ratio of two corresponding sides is known, then that ratio, or scale factor, holds true for all of the dimensions of the new figure.

Here is an example of applying this principle. Suppose that Lara is 5 feet tall and is standing 30 feet from the base of a light pole, and her shadow is 6 feet long. How high is the light on the pole? To figure this, it helps to make a sketch of the situation:

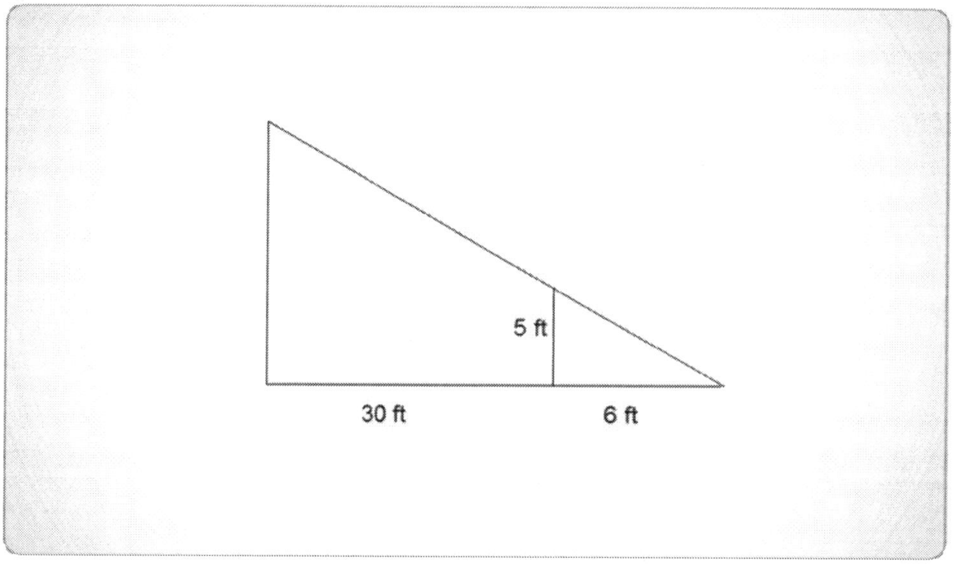

The light pole is the left side of the triangle. Lara is the 5-foot vertical line. Notice that there are two right triangles here, and that they have all the same angles as one another. Therefore, they form similar triangles. So, figure the ratio of proportionality between them.

The bases of these triangles are known. The small triangle, formed by Lara and her shadow, has a base of 6 feet. The large triangle, formed by the light pole along with the line from the base of the pole out to the end of Lara's shadow is $30 + 6 = 36$ feet long. So, the ratio of the big triangle to the little triangle will be $\frac{36}{6} = 6$. The height of the little triangle is 5 feet. Therefore, the height of the big triangle will be $6 \times 5 = 30$ feet, meaning that the light is 30 feet up the pole.

Notice that the perimeter of a figure changes by the ratio of proportionality between two similar figures, but the area changes by the *square* of the ratio. This is because if the length of one side is doubled, the area is quadrupled.

As an example, suppose two rectangles are similar, but the edges of the second rectangle are three times longer than the edges of the first rectangle. The area of the first rectangle is 10 square inches. How much more area does the second rectangle have than the first?

To answer this, note that the area of the second rectangle is $3^2 = 9$ times the area of the first rectangle, which is 10 square inches. Therefore, the area of the second rectangle is going to be $9 \times 10 = 90$ square inches. This means it has $90 - 10 = 80$ square inches more area than the first rectangle.

As a second example, suppose *X* and *Y* are similar right triangles. The hypotenuse of *X* is 4 inches. The area of *Y* is $\frac{1}{4}$ the area of *X*. What is the hypotenuse of *Y*?

First, realize the area has changed by a factor of $\frac{1}{4}$. The area changes by a factor that is the *square* of the ratio of changes in lengths, so the ratio of the lengths is the square root of the ratio of areas. That means that the ratio of lengths must be is $\sqrt{\frac{1}{4}} = \frac{1}{2}$, and the hypotenuse of *Y* must be $\frac{1}{2} \times 4 = 2$ inches.

Volumes between similar solids change like the cube of the change in the lengths of their edges. Likewise, if the ratio of the volumes between similar solids is known, the ratio between their lengths is known by finding the cube root of the ratio of their volumes.

For example, suppose there are two similar rectangular pyramids *X* and *Y*. The base of *X* is 1 inch by 2 inches, and the volume of *X* is 8 inches. The volume of *Y* is 64 inches. What are the dimensions of the base of *Y*?

To answer this, first find the ratio of the volume of *Y* to the volume of *X*. This will be given by $\frac{64}{8} = 8$. Now the ratio of lengths is the cube root of the ratio of volumes, or $\sqrt[3]{8} = 2$. So, the dimensions of the base of *Y* must be 2 inches by 4 inches.

Practice Questions

1. A ball is drawn at random from a ball pit containing 8 red balls, 7 yellow balls, 6 green balls, and 5 purple balls. What's the probability that the ball drawn is yellow?

   a. $\frac{1}{26}$

   b. $\frac{19}{26}$

   c. $\frac{7}{26}$

   d. 1

2. Two cards are drawn from a shuffled deck of 52 cards. What's the probability that both cards are Kings if the first card isn't replaced after it's drawn and is a King?

   a. $\frac{1}{169}$

   b. $\frac{1}{221}$

   c. $\frac{1}{13}$

   d. $\frac{4}{13}$

3. For a group of 20 men, the median weight is 180 pounds and the range is 30 pounds. If each man gains 10 pounds, which of the following would be true?

   a. The median weight will increase, and the range will remain the same.
   b. The median weight and range will both remain the same.
   c. The median weight will stay the same, and the range will increase.
   d. The median weight and range will both increase.

4. For the following similar triangles, what are the values of x and y (rounded to one decimal place)?

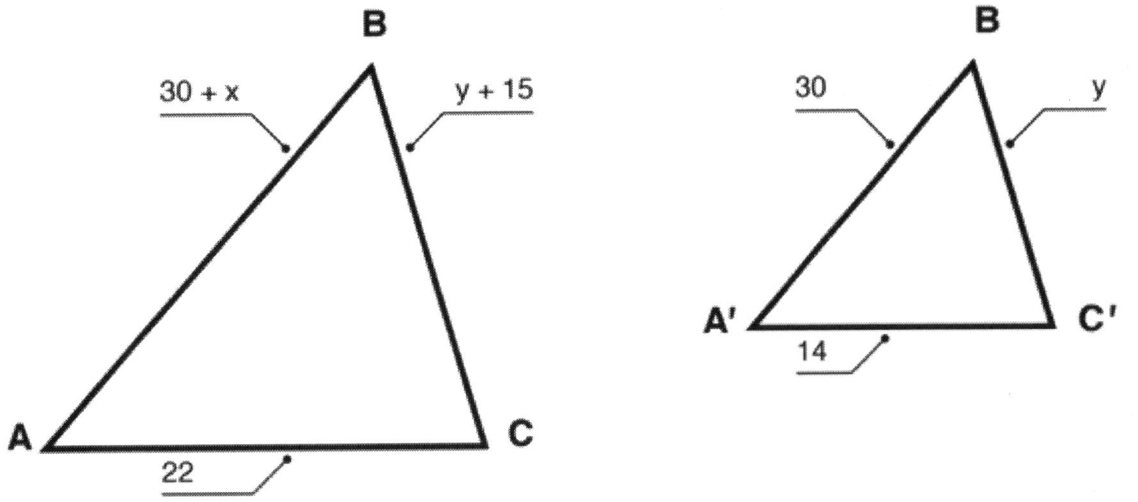

a. $x = 16.5, y = 25.1$
b. $x = 19.5, y = 24.1$
c. $x = 17.1, y = 26.3$
d. $x = 26.3, y = 17.1$

5. The triangle shown below is a right triangle. What's the value of x?

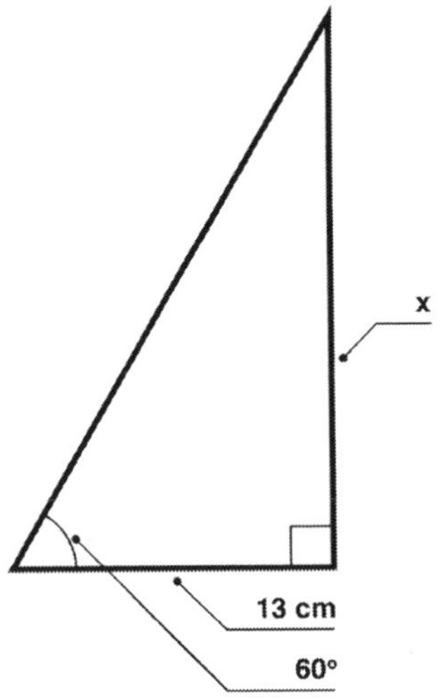

a. $x = 1.73$
b. $x = 0.57$
c. $x = 13$
d. $x = 22.49$

6. If $a \neq b$, solve for x if $\frac{1}{x} + \frac{2}{a} = \frac{2}{b}$

a. $\frac{a-b}{ab}$

b. $\frac{ab}{2(a-b)}$

c. $\frac{2(a-b)}{ab}$

d. $\frac{a-b}{2ab}$

7). $x = \frac{-1 \pm \sqrt{13}}{2}$

7. If $x^2 + x - 3 = 0$, then $\left(x - \frac{1}{2}\right)^2 =$

a. $\frac{11}{2}$

b. $\frac{11}{4}$

c. 11

d. $\frac{121}{4}$

8. Which graph will be a line parallel to the graph of $y = 3x - 2$?

a. $2y - 6x = 2$
b. $y - 4x = 4$
c. $3y = x - 2$
d. $2x - 2y = 2$

9. An equation for the line passing through the origin and the point $(2, 1)$ is

a. $y = 2x$
b. $y = \frac{1}{2}x$
c. $y = x - 2$
d. $2y = x + 1$

10. Jessica buys 10 cans of paint. Red paint costs \$1 per can and blue paint costs \$2 per can. In total, she spends \$16. How many red cans did she buy?

a. 2
b. 3
c. 4
d. 5

11. A farmer owns two (non-adjacent) square plots of land, which he wishes to fence. The area of one is 1000 square feet, while the area of the other is 10 square feet. How much fencing does he need, in feet?

a. 44
b. $40\sqrt{10}$
c. $440\sqrt{10}$
d. $44\sqrt{10}$

12. If $\log_{10} x = 2$, then *x* is

a. 4

b. 20

c. 100

d. 1000

13. $2x(3x+1) - 5(3x+1) =$

a. $10x(3x+1)$

b. $10x^2(3x+1)$

c. $(2x-5)(3x+1)$

d. $(2x+1)(3x-5)$

14. A root of $x^2 - 2x - 2$ is

a. $1+\sqrt{3}$

b. $1+2\sqrt{2}$

c. $2+2\sqrt{3}$

d. $2-2\sqrt{3}$

15. In the *xy*-plane, the graph of $y = x^2 + 2$ and the circle with center $(0,1)$ and radius 1 have how many points of intersection?

a. 0

b. 1

c. 2

d. 3

16. A line goes through the point (-4, 0) and the point (0,2). What is the slope of the line?

a. 2

b. 4

c. $\frac{3}{2}$

d. $\frac{1}{2}$

17. How many different ways can we order the letters *a*, *b*, *c*?

a. 3

b. 6

c. 9

d. 12

18. Six people apply to work for Janice's company, but she only needs four workers. How many different groups of four employees can Janice choose?

a. 6

b. 10

c. 15

d. 36

19. Given the following triangle, what's the length of the missing side? Round the answer to the nearest tenth.

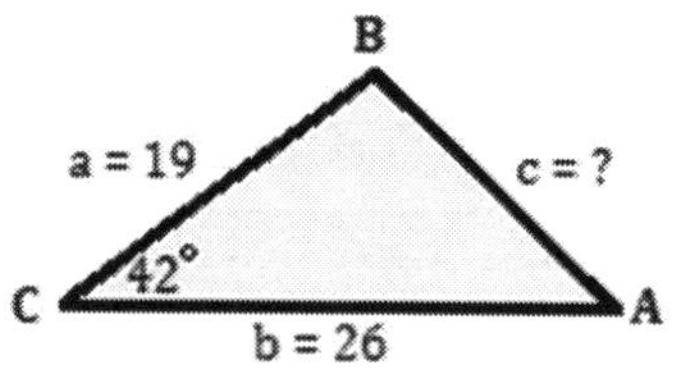

a. 17.0
b. 17.4
c. 18.0
d. 18.4

20. What are the coordinates of the focus of the parabola $y = -9x^2$?
a. $(-3, 0)$
b. $\left(-\frac{1}{36}, 0\right)$
c. $(0, -3)$
d. $\left(0, -\frac{1}{36}\right)$

Answer Explanations

1. C: The sample space is made up of $8 + 7 + 6 + 5 = 26$ balls. The probability of pulling each individual ball is $\frac{1}{26}$. Since there are 7 yellow balls, the probability of pulling a yellow ball is $\frac{7}{26}$.

2. B: For the first card drawn, the probability of a King being pulled is $\frac{4}{52}$. Since this card isn't replaced, if a King is drawn first, the probability of a King being drawn second is $\frac{3}{51}$. The probability of a King being drawn in both the first and second draw is the product of the two probabilities: $\frac{4}{52} \times \frac{3}{51} = \frac{12}{2{,}652}$ which, divided by 12, equals $\frac{1}{221}$.

3. A: If each man gains 10 pounds, every original data point will increase by 10 pounds. Therefore, the man with the original median will still have the median value, but that value will increase by 10. The smallest value and largest value will also increase by 10 and, therefore, the difference between the two won't change. The range does not change in value and, thus, remains the same.

4. C: Because the triangles are similar, the lengths of the corresponding sides are proportional. Therefore:

$$\frac{30 + x}{30} = \frac{22}{14} = \frac{y + 15}{y}$$

This results in the equation $14(30 + x) = 22 \times 30$ which, when solved, gives $x = 17.1$. The proportion also results in the equation $14(y + 15) = 22y$ which, when solved, gives $y = 26.3$.

11. D: SOHCAHTOA is used to find the missing side length. Because the angle and adjacent side are known, $\tan 60 = \frac{\text{x}}{13}$. Making sure to evaluate tangent with an argument in degrees, this equation gives:

$$x = 13 \tan 60 = 13 \times 1.73 = 22.49$$

5. B: The determinant of a 2 x 2 matrix is $ad - bc$. The calculation is -4(-1) – 2(3) = 4 – 6 = -2.

6. B: $\frac{2}{a}$ must be subtracted from both sides, with a result of $\frac{1}{x} = \frac{2}{b} - \frac{2}{a}$. The reciprocal of both sides needs to be taken, but the right-hand side needs to be written as a single fraction in order to do that. Since the two fractions on the right have denominators that are not equal, a common denominator of *ab* is needed. This leaves:

$$\frac{1}{x} = \frac{2a}{ab} - \frac{2b}{ab} = \frac{2(a - b)}{ab}$$

Taking the reciprocals, which can be done since *b* – *a* is not zero, with a result of $x = \frac{ab}{2(a-b)}$.

7. B: Plugging into the quadratic formula yields, for solutions:

$$x = \frac{1 \pm \sqrt{-1 + 4 \times 1(-3)}}{2} = \frac{1}{2} \pm \frac{\sqrt{11}}{2}$$

Therefore, $x - \frac{1}{2} = \pm\frac{\sqrt{11}}{2}$. Now, if this is squared, then the $\pm$ cancels and left with $\left(\frac{\sqrt{11}}{2}\right)^2 = \frac{11}{4}$.

8. A: Parallel lines have the same slope. The slope of *C* can be seen to be 1/3 by dividing both sides by 3. For *E*, divide both sides by 2 and see the slope is 3/2. The others are in standard form $Ax + By = C$, for which the slope is given by $\frac{-A}{B}$. The slope of *A* is 3, the slope of *B* is 4. The slope of *D* is 1.

9. B: The slope will be given by $\frac{1-0}{2-0} = \frac{1}{2}$. The *y*-intercept will be 0, since it passes through the origin. Using slope-intercept form, the equation for this line is $y = \frac{1}{2}x$.

10. C: Let *r* be the number of red cans and *b* be the number of blue cans. One equation is $r + b = 10$. The total price is $16, and the prices for each can means $1r + 2b = 16$. Multiplying the first equation on both sides by -1 results in $-r - b = -10$. Add this equation to the second equation, leaving $b = 6$. So, she bought 6 *blue* cans. From the first equation, this means *r* = 4; thus, she bought 4 *red* cans.

11. D: The first field has an area of 1000 feet, so the length of one side is $\sqrt{1000} = 10\sqrt{10}$. Since there are four sides to a square, the total perimeter is $40\sqrt{10}$. The second square has an area of 10 square feet, so the length of one side is $\sqrt{10}$, and the total perimeter is $4\sqrt{10}$. Adding these together gives:

$$40\sqrt{10} + 4\sqrt{10} = (40 + 4)\sqrt{10} = 44\sqrt{10}$$

12. C: If $\log_{10} x = 2$, then $10^2 = x$, which equals 100.

13. C: The $(3x + 1)$ can be factored to get $(2x - 5)(3x + 1)$.

14. A: Check each value, but it is easiest to use the quadratic formula, which gives:

$$x = \frac{2 \pm \sqrt{(-2)^2 - 4(1)(-2)}}{2} = 1 \pm \frac{\sqrt{12}}{2} = 1 \pm \frac{2\sqrt{3}}{2} = 1 \pm \sqrt{3}$$

The only one of these which appears as an answer choice is $1 + \sqrt{3}$.

15. B: The *y* coordinate of every point on the graph of $y = x^2 + 2$ has a vertex at (0,2) on the y-axis. The circle with a center at (0,1) also lies on the y-axis. With a radius of 1, the circle touches the parabola at one point. The vertex of the parabola (0,2).

16. D: The slope is given by the change in *y* divided by the change in *x*. The change in *y* is 2-0 = 2, and the change in *x* is 0 – (-4) = 4. The slope is $\frac{2}{4} = \frac{1}{2}$.

17. B: The number of ways to order *n* objects is given by the product $\binom{n}{1}\binom{n-1}{1} \dots \binom{1}{1}$. This is:

$$\binom{3}{1}\binom{2}{1}\binom{1}{1} = \frac{3!}{1!\,2!} \times \frac{2!}{1!\,1!} \times \frac{1!}{1!\,1!}$$

1! is just 1, and the 2! in the numerator and denominator will cancel one another, with a result of $3! = 3 \times 2 \times 1 = 6$.

18. C: Janice will be choosing 4 employees out of a set of 6 applicants, so this will be given by the choice function. The following equation shows the choice function worked out:

$$\binom{6}{4} = \frac{6!}{4!\,(6-4)!} = \frac{6!}{4!\,(2)!} = \frac{6 \times 5 \times 4 \times 3 \times 2 \times 1}{4 \times 3 \times 2 \times 1 \times 2 \times 1} = \frac{6 \times 5}{2} = 15$$

19. B: Because this isn't a right triangle, SOHCAHTOA can't be used. However, the law of cosines can be used. Therefore:

$$c^2 = a^2 + b^2 - 2ab\ \cos C = 19^2 + 26^2 - 2 \times 19 \times 26 \times \cos 42° = 302.773$$

Taking the square root and rounding to the nearest tenth results in $c = 17.4$.

20. D: A parabola of the form $y = \frac{1}{4f}x^2$ has a focus $(0, f)$. Because $y = -9x^2$, set $-9 = \frac{1}{4f}$. Solving this equation for f results in $f = -\frac{1}{36}$. Therefore, the coordinates of the focus are $\left(0, -\frac{1}{36}\right)$.

Advanced Algebra and Functions (AAF)

Factoring

Factors for polynomials are similar to factors for integers—they are numbers, variables, or polynomials that, when multiplied together, give a product equal to the polynomial in question. One polynomial is a factor of a second polynomial if the second polynomial can be obtained from the first by multiplying by a third polynomial.

$6x^6 + 13x^4 + 6x^2$ can be obtained by multiplying together $(3x^4 + 2x^2)(2x^2 + 3)$. This means $2x^2 + 3$ and $3x^4 + 2x^2$ are factors of $6x^6 + 13x^4 + 6x^2$.

In general, finding the factors of a polynomial can be tricky. However, there are a few types of polynomials that can be factored in a straightforward way.

If a certain monomial divides each term of a polynomial, it can be factored out:

$$x^2 + 2xy + y^2 = (x + y)^2$$

$$x^2 - 2xy + y^2 = (x - y)^2$$

$$x^2 - y^2 = (x + y)(x - y)$$

$$x^3 + y^3 = (x + y)(x^2 - xy + y^2)$$

$$x^3 - y^3 = (x - y)(x^2 + xy + y^2)$$

$$x^3 + 3x^2y + 3xy^2 + y^3 = (x + y)^3$$

$$x^3 - 3x^2y + 3xy^2 - y^3 = (x - y)^3$$

These rules can be used in many combinations with one another. For example, the expression:

$$3x^3 - 24$$

factors to:

$$3(x^3 - 8) = 3(x - 2)(x^2 + 2x + 4)$$

When factoring polynomials, a good strategy is to multiply the factors to check the result.

Quadratics

A polynomial of degree 2 is called *quadratic*. Every quadratic function can be written in the form $ax^2 + bx + c$. The graph of a quadratic function, $y = ax^2 + bx + c$, is called a *parabola*. Parabolas are vaguely U-shaped.

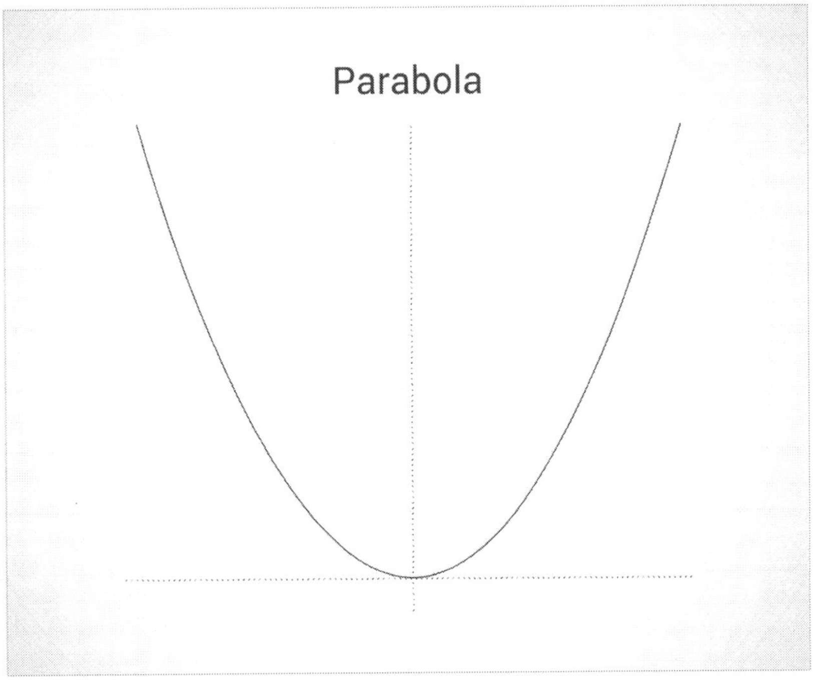

Whether the parabola opens upward or downward depends on the sign of *a*. If *a* is positive, then the parabola will open upward. If *a* is negative, then the parabola will open downward. The value of *a* will also affect how wide the parabola is. If the absolute value of *a* is large, then the parabola will be fairly skinny. If the absolute value of *a* is small, then the parabola will be quite wide.

Changes to the value of *b* affect the parabola in different ways, depending on the sign of *a*. For positive values of *a*, increasing *b* will move the parabola to the left, and decreasing *b* will move the parabola to the right. On the other hand, if *a* is negative, the effects will be the opposite: increasing *b* will move the parabola to the right, while decreasing *b* will move the parabola to the left.

Changes to the value of *c* move the parabola vertically. The larger that *c* is, the higher the parabola gets. This does not depend on the value of *a*.

The quantity $D = b^2 - 4ac$ is called the *discriminant* of the parabola. When the discriminant is positive, then the parabola has two real zeros, or *x* intercepts. However, if the discriminant is negative, then there are no real zeros, and the parabola will not cross the *x*-axis. The highest or lowest point of the parabola is called the *vertex*. If the discriminant is zero, then the parabola's highest or lowest point is on the *x*-axis, and it will have a single real zero. The x-coordinate of the vertex can be found using the equation $x = -\frac{b}{2a}$. Plug this x-value into the equation and find the y-coordinate.

A quadratic equation is often used to model the path of an object thrown into the air. The x-value can represent the time in the air, while the y-value can represent the height of the object. In this case, the maximum height of the object would be the y-value found when the x-value is $-\frac{b}{2a}$.

Solving Quadratic Equations

A *quadratic equation* is an equation in the form $ax^2 + bx + c = 0$. There are several methods to solve such equations. The easiest method will depend on the quadratic equation in question.

It sometimes is possible to solve quadratic equations by manually *factoring* them. This means rewriting them in the form $(x + A)(x + B) = 0$. If this is done, then they can be solved by remembering that when $ab = 0$, either *a* or *b* must be equal to zero. Therefore, to have $(x + A)(x + B) = 0$, $(x + A) = 0$ or $(x + B) = 0$ is needed. These equations have the solutions $x = -A$ and $x = -B$, respectively.

In order to factor a quadratic equation, note that $(x + A)(x + B) = x^2 + (A + B)x + AB$. So, if an equation is in the form $x^2 + bx + c$, two numbers, *A* and *B*, need to be found that will add up to give us *b*, and multiply together to give us *c*.

As an example, consider solving the equation $-3x^2 + 6x + 9 = 0$. Start by dividing both sides by -3, leaving $x^2 - 2x - 3 = 0$. Now, notice that $1 - 3 = -2$, and also that $(1)(-3) = -3$. This means the equation can be factored into $(x + 1)(x - 3) = 0$. Now, solve $(x + 1) = 0$ and $(x - 3) = 0$ to get $x = -1$ and $x = 3$ as the solutions.

It is useful when trying to factor to remember that:

$$x^2 + 2xy + y^2 = (x + y)^2, x^2 - 2xy + y^2 = (x - y)^2$$

$$x^2 - y^2 = (x + y)(x - y)$$

However, factoring by hand is often hard to do. If there are no obvious ways to factor the quadratic equation, solutions can still be found by using the *quadratic formula*.

The quadratic formula is:

$$x = \frac{-b \pm \sqrt{b^2 - 4ac}}{2a}$$

This method will always work, although it sometimes can take longer than factoring by hand, if the factors are easy to guess. Using the standard form $ax^2 + bx + c = 0$, plug the values of *a*, *b*, and *c* from the equation into the formula and solve for x. There will either be two answers, one answer, or no real answer. No real answer comes when the value of the discriminant, the number under the square root, is a negative number. Since there are no real numbers that square to get a negative, the answer will be no real roots.

Here is an example of solving a quadratic equation using the quadratic formula. Suppose the equation to solve is $-2x^2 + 3x + 1 = 0$. There is no obvious way to factor this, so the quadratic formula is used, with $a = -2, b = 3, c = 1$. After substituting these values into the quadratic formula, it yields this:

$$x = \frac{-3 \pm \sqrt{3^2 - 4(-2)(1)}}{2(-2)}$$

This can be simplified to obtain:

$$\frac{3 \pm \sqrt{9+8}}{4}$$

or

$$\frac{3 \pm \sqrt{17}}{4}$$

Challenges can be encountered when asked to find a quadratic equation with specific roots. Given roots *A* and *B*, a quadratic function can be constructed with those roots by taking $(x - A)(x - B)$. So, in constructing a quadratic equation with roots $x = -2, 3$, it would result in $(x + 2)(x - 3) = x^2 - x - 6$. Multiplying this by a constant also could be done without changing the roots.

Functions

A *function* is defined as a relationship between inputs and outputs where there is only one output value for a given input. As an example, the following function is in function notation: $f(x) = 3x - 4$. The $f(x)$ represents the output value for an input of x. If $x = 2$, the equation becomes:

$$f(2) = 3(2) - 4 = 6 - 4 = 2$$

The input of 2 yields an output of 2, forming the ordered pair $(2, 2)$. The following set of ordered pairs corresponds to the given function: $(2, 2), (0, -4), (-2, -10)$. The set of all possible inputs of a function is its *domain*, and all possible outputs is called the *range*. By definition, each member of the domain is paired with only one member of the range.

Functions can also be defined recursively. In this form, they are not defined explicitly in terms of variables. Instead, they are defined using previously-evaluated function outputs, starting with either $f(0)$ or $f(1)$. An example of a recursively-defined function is:

$$f(1) = 2, f(n) = 2f(n - 1) + 2n, n > 1$$

The domain of this function is the set of all integers.

Domain and Range

The domain and range of a function can be found visually by its plot on the coordinate plane. In the function $f(x) = x^2 - 3$, for example, the domain is all real numbers because the parabola stretches as far left and as far right as it can go, with no restrictions. This means that any input value from the real number system will yield an answer in the real number system. For the range, the inequality $y \geq -3$ would be used to describe the possible output values because the parabola has a minimum at $y = -3$. This means there will not be any real output values less than -3 because -3 is the lowest value it reaches on the y-axis.

These same answers for domain and range can be found by observing a table. The table below shows that from input values $x = -1$ to $x = 1$, the output results in a minimum of -3. On each side of $x = 0$, the numbers increase, showing that the range is all real numbers greater than or equal to -3.

x (domain/input)	y (range/output)
-2	1
-1	-2
0	-3
-1	-2
2	1

Function Behavior

Different types of functions behave in different ways. A function is defined to be increasing over a subset of its domain if for all $x_1 \geq x_2$ in that interval, $f(x_1) \geq f(x_2)$. Also, a function is decreasing over an interval if for all $x_1 \geq x_2$ in that interval, $f(x_1) \leq f(x_2)$. A point in which a function changes from increasing to decreasing can also be labeled as the *maximum value* of a function if it is the largest point the graph reaches on the y-axis. A point in which a function changes from decreasing to increasing can be labeled as the minimum value of a function if it is the smallest point the graph reaches on the y-axis. Maximum values are also known as *extreme values*. The graph of a continuous function does not have any breaks or jumps in the graph. This description is not true of all functions. A radical function, for example, $f(x) = \sqrt{x}$, has a restriction for the domain and range because there are no real negative inputs or outputs for this function. The domain can be stated as $x \geq 0$, and the range is $y \geq 0$.

A piecewise-defined function also has a different appearance on the graph. In the following function, there are three equations defined over different intervals. It is a function because there is only one y-value for each x-value, passing the Vertical Line Test. The domain is all real numbers less than or equal to 6. The range is all real numbers greater than zero. From left to right, the graph decreases to zero, then increases to almost 4, and then jumps to 6.

From input values greater than 2, the input decreases just below 8 to 4, and then stops.

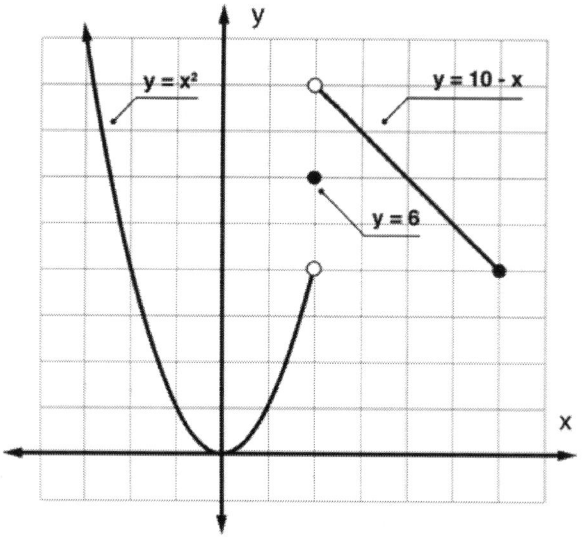

Logarithmic and exponential functions also have different behavior than other functions. These two types of functions are inverses of each other. The *inverse* of a function can be found by switching the place of x and y, and solving for y. When this is done for the exponential equation, $y = 2^x$, the function $y = \log_2 x$ is found. The general form of a *logarithmic function* is $y = log_b x$, which says b raised to the y power equals x.

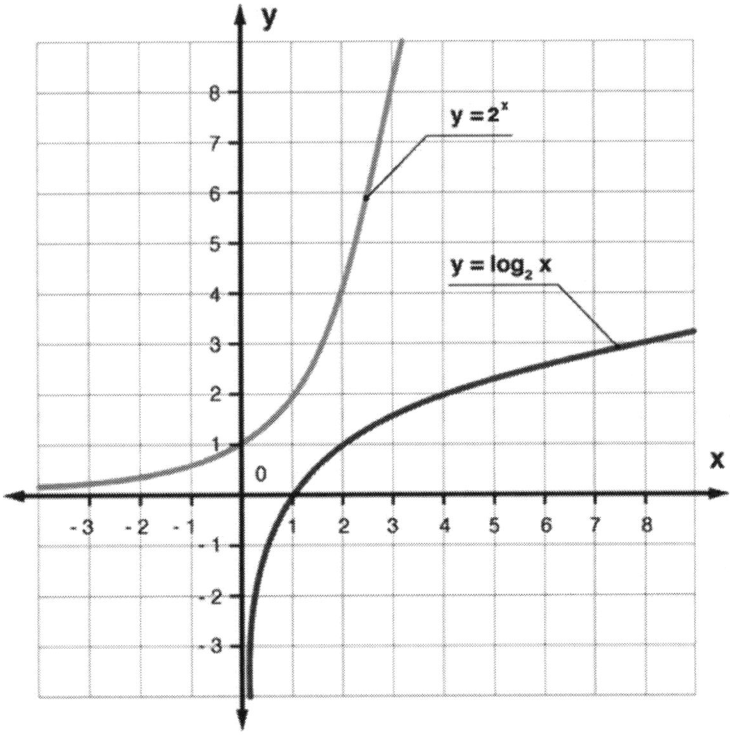

The thick black line on the graph above represents the logarithmic function $y = \log_2 x$. This curve passes through the point $(1, 0)$, just as all log functions do, because any value $b^0 = 1$. The graph of this logarithmic function starts very close to zero, but does not touch the y-axis. The output value will never be zero by the definition of logarithms. The thinner gray line seen above represents the exponential function $y = 2^x$. The behavior of this function is opposite the logarithmic function because the graph of an inverse function is the graph of the original function flipped over the line $y = x$. The curve passes through the point $(0, 1)$ because any number raised to the zero power is one. This curve also gets very close to the x-axis but never touches it because an exponential expression never has an output of zero. The x-axis on this graph is called a horizontal asymptote. An *asymptote* is a line that represents a boundary for a function. It shows a value that the function will get close to, but never reach.

Functions can also be described as being even, odd, or neither. If $f(-x) = f(x)$, the function is even. For example, the function $f(x) = x^2 - 2$ is even. Plugging in $x = 2$ yields an output of $y = 2$. After changing the input to $x = -2$, the output is still $y = 2$. The output is the same for opposite inputs. Another way to observe an even function is by the symmetry of the graph. If the graph is symmetrical about the axis, then the function is even. If the graph is symmetric about the origin, then the function is odd. Algebraically, if $f(-x) = -f(x)$, the function is odd.

Also, a function can be described as periodic if it repeats itself in regular intervals. Common periodic functions are trigonometric functions. For example, $y = \sin x$ is a periodic function with period 2π because it repeats itself every 2π units along the x-axis.

Building a Function

Functions can be built out of the context of a situation. For example, the relationship between the money paid for a gym membership and the months that someone has been a member can be described through a function. If the one-time membership fee is \$40 and the monthly fee is \$30, then the function can be written $f(x) = 30x + 40$. The x-value represents the number of months the person has been part of the gym, while the output is the total money paid for the membership. The table below shows this relationship. It is a representation of the function because the initial cost is \$40 and the cost increases each month by \$30.

x (months)	y (money paid to gym)
0	40
1	70
2	100
3	130

Functions can also be built from existing functions. For example, a given function $f(x)$ can be transformed by adding a constant, multiplying by a constant, or changing the input value by a constant. The new function $g(x) = f(x) + k$ represents a vertical shift of the original function. In $f(x) = 3x - 2$, a vertical shift 4 units up would be:

$$g(x) = 3x - 2 + 4 = 3x + 2$$

Multiplying the function times a constant k represents a vertical stretch, based on whether the constant is greater than or less than 1. The function

$$g(x) = kf(x) = 4(3x - 2) = 12x - 8$$

represents a stretch. Changing the input x by a constant forms the function:

$$g(x) = f(x + k) = 3(x + 4) - 2 = 3x + 12 - 2 = 3x + 10$$

This represents a horizontal shift to the left 4 units. If $(x - 4)$ was plugged into the function, it would represent a vertical shift.

A composition function can also be formed by plugging one function into another. In function notation, this is written:

$$(f \circ g)(x) = f(g(x))$$

For two functions $f(x) = x^2$ and $g(x) = x - 3$, the composition function becomes:

$$f\big(g(x)\big) = (x - 3)^2 = x^2 - 6x + 9$$

The composition of functions can also be used to verify if two functions are inverses of each other. Given the two functions $f(x) = 2x + 5$ and $g(x) = \frac{x-5}{2}$, the composition function can be found $(f \circ g)(x)$. Solving this equation yields:

$$f\big(g(x)\big) = 2\left(\frac{x - 5}{2}\right) + 5 = x - 5 + 5 = x$$

It also is true that $g(f(x)) = x$. Since the composition of these two functions gives a simplified answer of x, this verifies that $f(x)$ and $g(x)$ are inverse functions. The domain of $f(g(x))$ is the set of all x-values in the domain of $g(x)$ such that $g(x)$ is in the domain of $f(x)$. Basically, both $f(g(x))$ and $g(x)$ have to be defined.

To build an inverse of a function, $f(x)$ needs to be replaced with y, and the x and y values need to be switched. Then, the equation can be solved for y. For example, given the equation $y = e^{2x}$, the inverse can be found by rewriting the equation $x = e^{2y}$. The natural logarithm of both sides is taken down, and the exponent is brought down to form the equation:

$$\ln(x) = \ln(e)\,2y$$

$\ln(e)$=1, which yields the equation $\ln(x) = 2y$. Dividing both sides by 2 yields the inverse equation

$$\frac{\ln(x)}{2} = y = f^{-1}(x)$$

The domain of an inverse function is the range of the original function, and the range of an inverse function is the domain of the original function. Therefore, an ordered pair (x, y) on either a graph or a table corresponding to $f(x)$ means that the ordered pair (y, x) exists on the graph of $f^{-1}(x)$. Basically, if $f(x) = y$, then $f^{-1}(y) = x$. For a function to have an inverse, it must be one-to-one. That means it must pass the *Horizontal Line Test*, and if any horizontal line passes through the graph of the function twice, a function is not one-to-one. The domain of a function that is not one-to-one can be restricted to an interval in which the function is one-to-one, to be able to define an inverse function.

Functions can also be formed from combinations of existing functions.

Given $f(x)$ and $g(x)$, the following can be built:

$$f + g$$

$$f - g$$

$$fg$$

$$\frac{f}{g}$$

The domains of $f + g, f - g,$ and fg are the intersection of the domains of f and g. The domain of $\frac{f}{g}$ is the same set, excluding those values that make $g(x) = 0$.

For example, if:

$$f(x) = 2x + 3$$

$$g(x) = x + 1$$

then

$$\frac{f}{g} = \frac{2x + 3}{x + 1}$$

Its domain is all real numbers except -1.

Common Functions

Three common functions used to model different relationships between quantities are linear, quadratic, and exponential functions. Linear functions are the simplest of the three, and the independent variable x has an exponent of 1. Written in the most common form, $y = mx + b$, the coefficient of x tells how fast the function grows at a constant rate, and the b-value tells the starting point. A quadratic function has an exponent of 2 on the independent variable x. Standard form for this type of function is $y = ax^2 + bx + c$, and the graph is a parabola. These type functions grow at a changing rate. An exponential function has an independent variable in the exponent $y = ab^x$. The graph of these types of functions is described as *growth* or *decay*, based on whether the base, b, is greater than or less than 1. These functions are different from quadratic functions because the base stays constant. A common base is base *e*.

The following three functions model a linear, quadratic, and exponential function respectively: $y = 2x$, $y = x^2$, and $y = 2^x$. Their graphs are shown below. The first graph, modeling the linear function, shows that the growth is constant over each interval. With a horizontal change of 1, the vertical change is 2. It models a constant positive growth. The second graph shows the quadratic function, which is a curve that is symmetric across the y-axis. The growth is not constant, but the change is mirrored over the axis. The last graph models the exponential function, where the horizontal change of 1 yields a vertical change that increases more and more. The exponential graph gets very close to the x-axis, but never touches it, meaning there is an asymptote there. The y-value can never be zero because the base of 2 can never be raised to an input value that yields an output of zero.

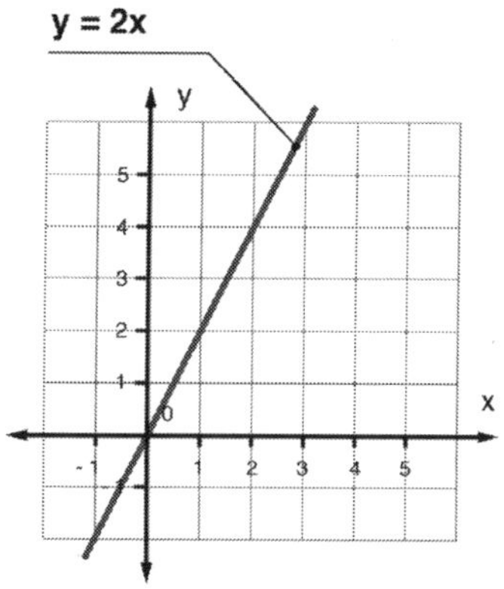

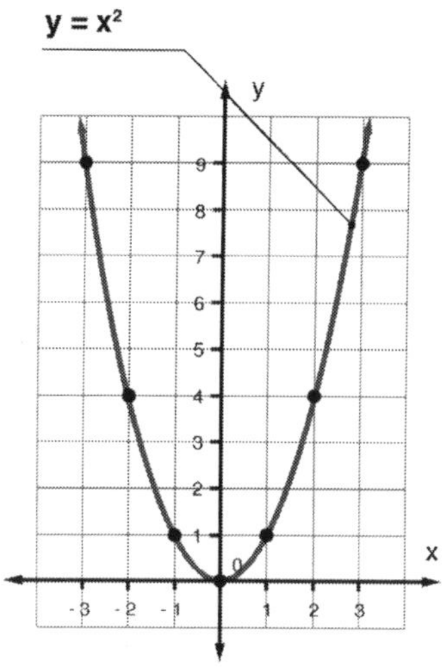

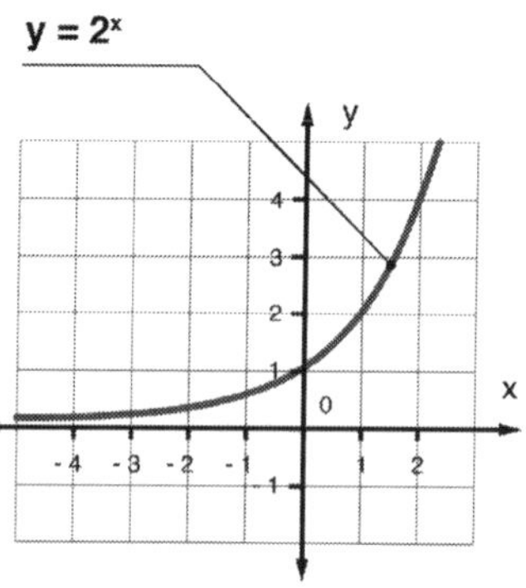

The three tables below show specific values for three types of functions. The third column in each table shows the change in the y-values for each interval. The first table shows a constant change of 2 for each equal interval, which matches the slope in the equation $y = 2x$. The second table shows an increasing change, but it also has a pattern. The increase is changing by 2 more each time, so the change is quadratic. The third table shows the change as factors of the base, 2. It shows a continuing pattern of factors of the base.

y = 2x		
x	y	Δy
1	2	
2	4	2
3	6	2
4	8	2
5	10	2

$y = x^2$		
x	y	Δy
1	1	
2	4	3
3	9	5
4	16	7
5	25	9

$y = 2^x$		
x	y	Δy
1	2	
2	4	2
3	8	4
4	16	8
5	32	16

Given a table of values, the type of function can be determined by observing the change in y over equal intervals. For example, the tables below model two functions. The changes in interval for the x-values is 1 for both tables. For the first table, the y-values increase by 5 for each interval. Since the change is constant, the situation can be described as a linear function. The equation would be $y = 5x + 3$. For the second table, the change for y is 5, 20, 100, and 500, respectively. The increases are multiples of 5, meaning the situation can be modeled by an exponential function. The equation $y = 5^x + 3$ models this situation.

x	y
0	3
1	8
2	13
3	18
4	23

x	y
0	3
1	8
2	28
3	128
4	628

Quadratic equations can be used to model real-world area problems. For example, a farmer may have a rectangular field that he needs to sow with seed. The field has length $x + 8$ and width $2x$. The formula for area should be used: $A = lw$. Therefore:

$$A = (x + 8) * 2x = 2x^2 + 16x$$

The possible values for the length and width can be shown in a table, with input x and output A. If the equation was graphed, the possible area values can be seen on the y-axis for given x-values.

Exponential growth and decay can be found in real-world situations. For example, if a piece of notebook paper is folded 25 times, the thickness of the paper can be found. To model this situation, a table can be used. The initial point is one-fold, which yields a thickness of 2 papers. For the second fold, the thickness is 4. Since the thickness doubles each time, the table below shows the thickness for the next few folds. Notice the thickness changes by the same factor each time. Since this change for a constant interval of folds is a factor of 2, the function is exponential. The equation for this is $y = 2^x$. For twenty-five folds, the thickness would be 33,554,432 papers.

x (folds)	y (paper thickness)
0	1
1	2
2	4
3	8
4	16
5	32

One exponential formula that is commonly used is the *interest formula*: $A = Pe^{rt}$. In this formula, interest is compounded continuously. A is the value of the investment after the time, t, in years. P is the initial amount of the investment, r is the interest rate, and e is the constant equal to approximately 2.718. Given an initial amount of $200 and a time of 3 years, if interest is compounded continuously at a rate of 6%, the total investment value can be found by plugging each value into the formula. The invested value at the end is $239.44. In more complex problems, the final investment may be given, and the rate may be the unknown. In this case, the formula becomes $239.44 = 200e^{r3}$. Solving for r requires isolating the exponential expression on one side by dividing by 200, yielding the equation $1.20 = e^{r3}$. Taking the natural log of both sides results in $\ln(1.2) = r3$. Using a calculator to evaluate the logarithmic expression, $r = 0.06 = 6\%$.

When working with logarithms and exponential expressions, it is important to remember the relationship between the two. In general, the logarithmic form is $y = log_b x$ for an exponential form $b^y = x$. Logarithms and exponential functions are inverses of each other.

Odd, Even, and Monotone Functions

A function is called *monotone* if it is either always increasing or always decreasing. For example, the functions $f(x) = 3x$ and $f(x) = -x^5$ are monotone.

An *even function* looks the same when flipped over the *y*-axis: $f(x) = f(-x)$. The following image shows a graphic representation of an even function.

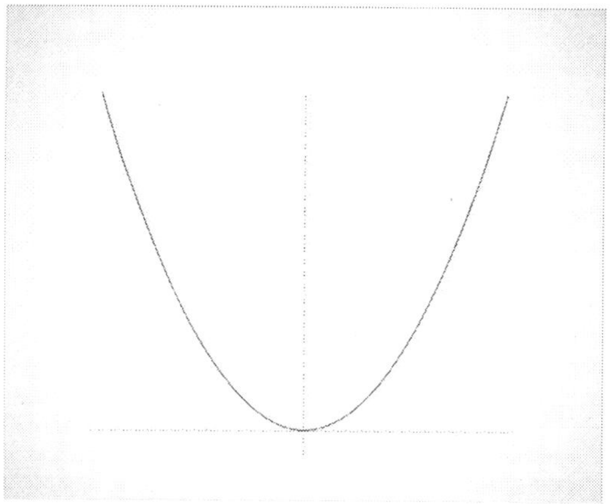

An *odd function* looks the same when flipped over the *y*-axis and then flipped over the *x*-axis: $f(x) = -f(-x)$. The following image shows an example of an odd function.

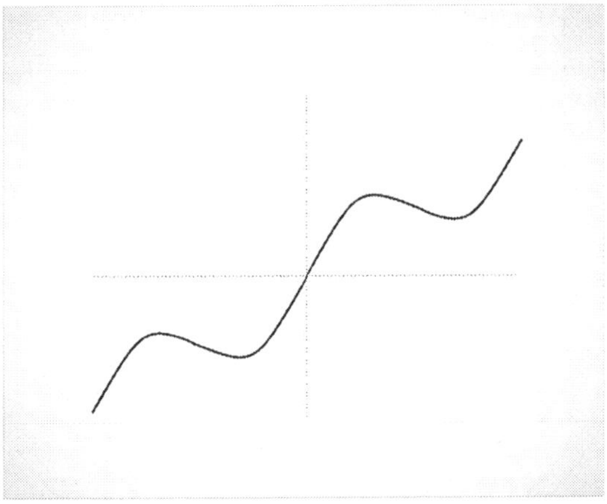

Radical and Rational Equations

Rational Expressions

A rational expression is a fraction where the numerator and denominator are both polynomials. Some examples of rational expressions include the following: $\frac{4x^3y^5}{3z^4}$, $\frac{4x^3+3x}{x^2}$, and $\frac{x^2+7x+10}{x+2}$. Since these refer to expressions and not equations, they can be simplified but not solved. Using the rules in the previous Exponents and Roots sections, some rational expressions with monomials can be simplified. Other rational expressions such as the last example, $\frac{x^2+7x+10}{x+2}$, take more steps to be simplified. First, the polynomial on top can be factored from $x^2 + 7x + 10$ into $(x + 5)(x + 2)$. Then the common factors can be canceled and the expression can be simplified to $(x + 5)$.

Consider this problem as an example of using rational expressions. Reggie wants to lay sod in his rectangular backyard. The length of the yard is given by the expression $4x + 2$ and the width is unknown. The area of the yard is $20x + 10$. Reggie needs to find the width of the yard. Knowing that the area of a rectangle is length multiplied by width, an expression can be written to find the width: $\frac{20x+10}{4x+2}$, area divided by length. Simplifying this expression by factoring out 10 on the top and 2 on the bottom leads to this expression: $\frac{10(2x+1)}{2(2x+1)}$. By cancelling out the $2x + 1$, that results in $\frac{10}{2} = 5$. The width of the yard is found to be 5 by simplifying a rational expression.

Rational Equations

A *rational equation* can be as simple as an equation with a ratio of polynomials, $\frac{p(x)}{q(x)}$, set equal to a value, where $p(x)$ and $q(x)$ are both polynomials. Notice that a rational equation has an equal sign, which is different from expressions. This leads to solutions, or numbers that make the equation true.

It is possible to solve rational equations by trying to get all of the *x* terms out of the denominator and then isolate them on one side of the equation. For example, to solve the equation $\frac{3x+2}{2x+3} = 4$, start by multiplying both sides by $(2x + 3)$. This will cancel on the left side to yield $3x + 2 = 4(2x + 3)$, then $3x + 2 = 8x + 12$. Now, subtract $8x$ from both sides, which yields $-5x + 2 = 12$. Subtracting 2 from both sides results in $-5x = 10$. Finally, divide both sides by -5 to obtain $x = -2$.

Sometimes, when solving rational equations, it can be easier to try to simplify the rational expression by factoring the numerator and denominator first, then cancelling out common factors. For example, to solve:

$$\frac{2x^2 - 8x + 6}{x^2 - 3x + 2} = 1$$

Start by factoring:

$$2x^2 - 8x + 6 = 2(x^2 - 4x + 3) = 2(x - 1)(x - 3)$$

Then, factor $x^2 - 3x + 2$ into $(x - 1)(x - 2)$. This turns the original equation into:

$$\frac{2(x - 1)(x - 3)}{(x - 1)(x - 2)} = 1$$

The common factor of $(x - 1)$ can be canceled, leaving us with $\frac{2(x-3)}{x-2} = 1$. Now the same method used in the previous example can be followed. Multiplying both sides by $x - 2$ and performing the multiplication on the left yields $2x - 6 = x - 2$, which can be simplified to $x = 4$.

Rational Functions

A rational function is similar to an equation, but it includes two variables. In general, a rational function is in the form: $f(x) = \frac{p(x)}{q(x)}$, where $p(x)$ and $q(x)$ are polynomials. Refer to the previous Functions section for a more detailed definition of functions. Rational functions are defined everywhere except where the denominator is equal to zero. When the denominator is equal to zero, this indicates either a hole in the graph or an asymptote. An asymptote can be either vertical, horizontal, or slant. A hole occurs when both the numerator and denominator are equal to 0 for a given value of *x*. A rational function can have at most one vertical asymptote and one horizontal or slant asymptote. An asymptote is a line such that the distance between the curve and the line tends toward 0, but never reaches it, as the line heads toward infinity. Examples of these types of functions are shown below. The first graph shows a rational function with a vertical asymptote at x = 0. This can be found by setting the denominator equal to 0. In this case it is just x = 0.

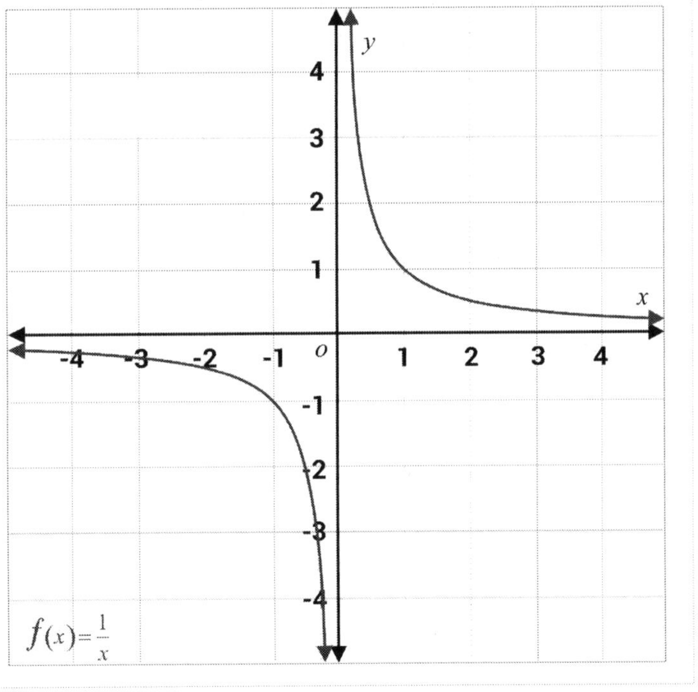

y
x
4
3
2
1
o
-4
-3
-2
-1
1
2
3
4
-1
-2
-3
-4
$f(x) = \frac{1}{x}$

The second graph shows a rational function with a vertical asymptote at x = -.5. Again this can be found by just setting the denominator equal to 0. So:

$$2x^2 + x = 0$$

$$2x + 1 = 0$$

$$2x = -1$$

$$x = -.5$$

This graph also has a hole in the graph at $x = 0$. This is because both the numerator and denominator are equal to 0 when $x = 0$.

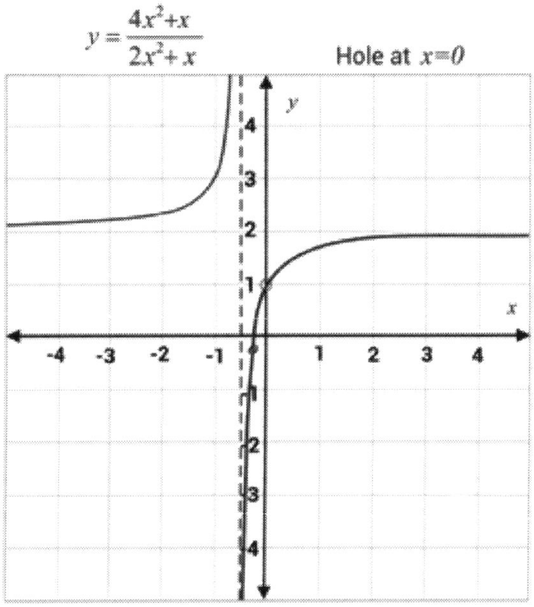

Polynomial Equations

An expression of the form ax^n, where *n* is a non-negative integer, is called a *monomial* because it contains one term. A sum of monomials is called a *polynomial*. For example, $-4x^3 + x$ is a polynomial, while $5x^7$ is a monomial. A function equal to a polynomial is called a *polynomial function*.

The monomials in a polynomial are also called the *terms* of the polynomial.

The constants that precede the variables are called *coefficients*.

The highest value of the exponent of *x* in a polynomial is called the *degree* of the polynomial. So, $-4x^3 + x$ has a degree of 3, while $-2x^5 + x^3 + 4x + 1$ has a degree of 5. When multiplying polynomials, the degree of the result will be the sum of the degrees of the two polynomials being multiplied.

To add polynomials, add the coefficients of like powers of *x*. For example:

$$(-2x^5 + x^3 + 4x + 1) + (-4x^3 + x) = -2x^5 + (1 - 4)x^3 + (4 + 1)x + 1 = -2x^5 - 3x^3 + 5x + 1$$

Likewise, subtraction of polynomials is performed by subtracting coefficients of like powers of *x*. So:

$$(-2x^5 + x^3 + 4x + 1) - (-4x^3 + x) = -2x^5 + (1 + 4)x^3 + (4 - 1)x + 1 = -2x^5 + 5x^3 + 3x + 1.$$

To multiply two polynomials, multiply each term of the first polynomial by each term of the second polynomial and add the results. For example:

$$(4x^2 + x)(-x^3 + x) = 4x^2(-x^3) + 4x^2(x) + x(-x^3) + x(x) = -4x^5 + 4x^3 - x^4 + x^2$$

In the case where each polynomial has two terms, like in this example, some students find it helpful to remember this as multiplying the First terms, then the Outer terms, then the Inner terms, and finally the Last terms, with the mnemonic FOIL. For longer polynomials, the multiplication process is the same, but there will be, of course, more terms, and there is no common mnemonic to remember each combination.

The process of *factoring* a polynomial means to write the polynomial as a product of other (generally simpler) polynomials. Here is an example:

$$x^2 - 4x + 3 = (x - 1)(x - 3)$$

If a certain monomial divides every term of the polynomial, factor it out of each term, for example:

$$4x^3 + 16x^2 = 4x^2(x + 4).$$

$$x^2 + 2xy + y^2 = (x + y)^2 \text{ or } x^2 - 2xy + y^2 = (x - y)^2$$

$$x^2 - y^2 = (x + y)(x - y)$$

$$x^3 + y^3 = (x + y)(x^2 - xy + y^2)$$

$$x^3 - y^3 = (x - y)(x^2 + xy + y^2)$$

$$x^3 + 3x^2y + 3xy^2 + y^3 = (x + y)^3 \text{ and } x^3 - 3x^2y + 3xy^2 - y^3 = (x - y)^3$$

It sometimes can be necessary to rewrite the polynomial in some clever way before applying the above rules. Consider the problem of factoring $x^4 - 1$. This does not immediately look like any of the cases for which there are rules. However, it's possible to think of this polynomial as:

$$x^4 - 1 = (x^2)^2 - (1^2)^2$$

Now apply the third rule in the above list to simplify this:

$$(x^2)^2 - (1^2)^2 = (x^2 + 1^2)(x^2 - 1^2) = (x^2 + 1)(x^2 - 1)$$

Exponential and Logarithmic Equations

A *logarithmic function* is an inverse for an exponential function. The inverse of the base *b* exponential function is written as $\log_b(x)$, and is called the *base b logarithm*. The domain of a logarithm is all positive real numbers. It has the properties that $\log_b(b^x) = x$. For positive real values of *x*, $b^{\log_b(x)} = x$.

When there is no chance of confusion, the parentheses are sometimes skipped for logarithmic functions: $\log_b(x)$ may be written as $\log_b x$. For the special number *e*, the base *e* logarithm is called the *natural logarithm* and is written as $\ln x$. Logarithms are one-to-one.

Solving Logarithmic and Exponential Functions

To solve an equation involving exponential expressions, the goal is to isolate the exponential expression. Once this process is completed, the logarithm—with the base equaling the base of the exponent of both sides—needs to be taken to get an expression for the variable. If the base is e, the natural log of both sides needs to be taken.

To solve an equation with logarithms, the given equation needs to be written in exponential form, using the fact that $\log_b y = x$ means $b^x = y$, and then solved for the given variable. Lastly, properties of logarithms can be used to simplify more than one logarithmic expression into one.

When working with logarithmic functions, it is important to remember the following properties. Each one can be derived from the definition of the logarithm as the inverse to an exponential function:

$$\log_b 1 = 0$$

$$\log_b b = 1$$

$$\log_b b^p = p$$

$$\log_b MN = \log_b M + \log_b N$$

$$\log_b \frac{M}{N} = \log_b M - \log_b N$$

$$\log_b M^p = p \log_b M$$

When solving equations involving exponentials and logarithms, the following fact should be used:

If f is a one-to-one function, $a = b$ is equivalent to $f(a) = f(b)$.

Using this, together with the fact that logarithms and exponentials are inverses, allows manipulations of the equations to isolate the variable.

<u>Example</u>
Solve $4 = \ln(x - 4)$.

Using the definition of a logarithm, the equation can be changed to $e^4 = e^{\ln(x-4)}$.

The functions on the right side cancel with a result of $e^4 = x - 4$.

This then gives $x = 4 + e^4$.

<u>Exponential Expressions</u>
Exponential expressions can also be rewritten, just as quadratic equations. Properties of exponents must be understood. Multiplying two exponential expressions with the same base involves adding the exponents:

$$a^m a^n = a^{m+n}$$

Dividing two exponential expressions with the same base involves subtracting the exponents:

$$\frac{a^m}{a^n} = a^{m-n}$$

Raising an exponential expression to another exponent includes multiplying the exponents:

$$(a^m)^n = a^{mn}$$

The zero power always gives a value of 1: $a^0 = 1$. Raising either a product or a fraction to a power involves distributing that power:

$$(ab)^m = a^m b^m \text{ and } \left(\frac{a}{b}\right)^m = \frac{a^m}{b^m}$$

Finally, raising a number to a negative exponent is equivalent to the reciprocal including the positive exponent:

$$a^{-m} = \frac{1}{a^m}$$

Trigonometry

Trigonometric functions are built out of two basic functions, the *sine* and *cosine*, written as $\sin\theta$ and $\cos\theta$ respectively. Note that similar to logarithms, it is customary to drop the parentheses as long as the result is not confusing.

The sine and cosine are defined using the *unit circle*. If θ is the angle going counterclockwise around the origin from the *x*-axis, then the point on the unit circle in that direction will have the coordinates $(\cos\theta, \sin\theta)$.

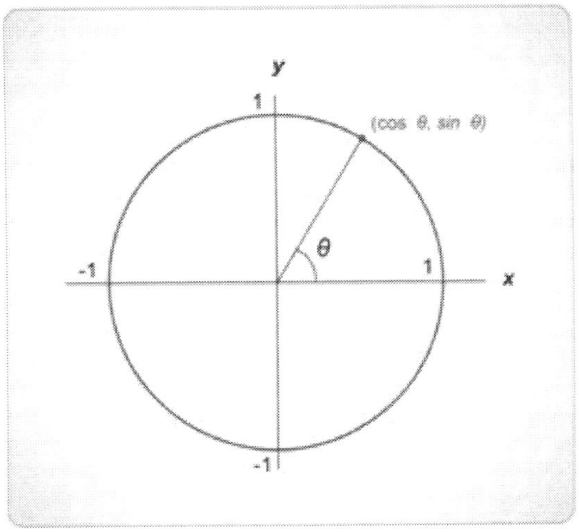

Since the angle returns to the start every 2π radians (or 360 degrees), the graph of these functions will be *periodic*, with period 2π. This means that the graph repeats itself as one moves along the *x*-axis because $\sin\theta = \sin(\theta + 2\pi)$. Cosine is works similarly.

From the unit circle definition, the sine function starts at 0 when $\theta = 0$. It grows to 1 as θ grows to $\pi/2$, and then back to 0 at $\theta = \pi$. Then it decreases to -1 as θ grows to $3\pi/2$, and back up to 0 at $\theta = 2\pi$.

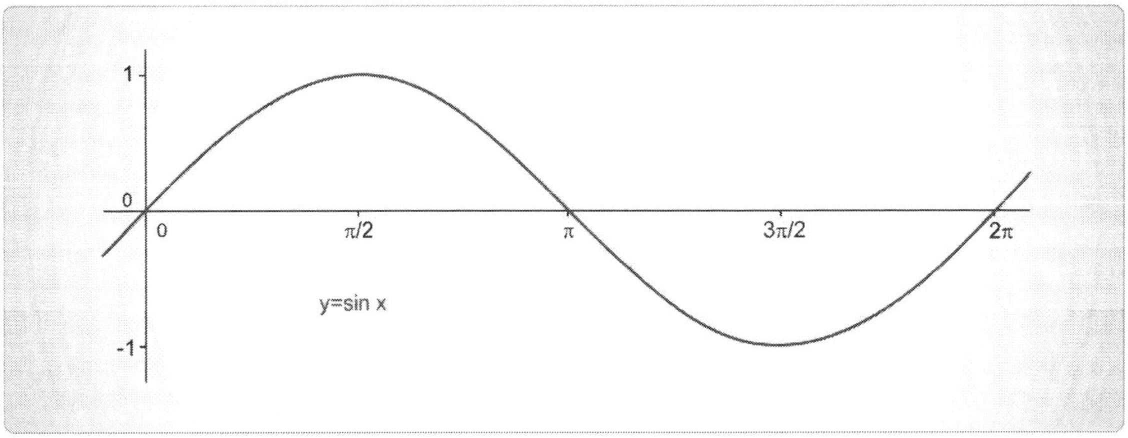

The graph of the cosine is similar. The cosine will start at 1, decreasing to 0 at $\pi/2$ and continuing to decrease to -1 at $\theta = \pi$. Then, it grows to 0 as θ grows to $3\pi/2$ and back up to 1 at $\theta = 2\pi$.

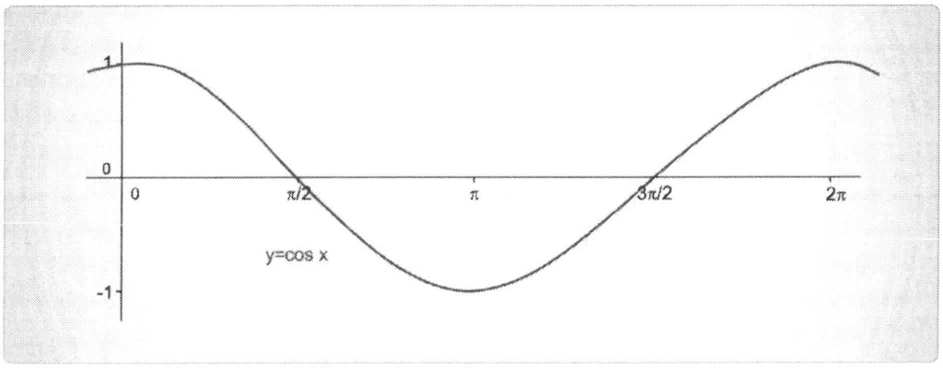

Another trigonometric function, which is frequently used, is the *tangent* function. This is defined as the following equation: $\tan\theta = \frac{\sin\theta}{\cos\theta}$.

The tangent function is a period of π rather than 2π because the sine and cosine functions have the same absolute values after a change in the angle of π, but flip their signs. Since the tangent is a ratio of the two functions, the changes in signs cancel.

The tangent function will be zero when the sine is zero, and it will have a vertical asymptote whenever cosine is zero. The following graph shows the tangent function:

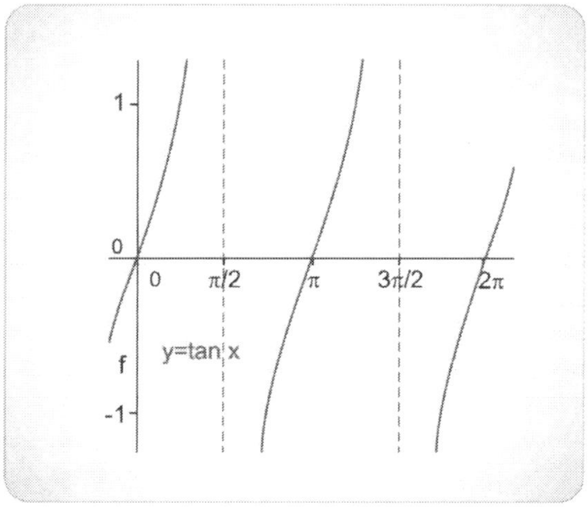

Three other trigonometric functions are sometimes useful. These are the *reciprocal* trigonometric functions, so named because they are just the reciprocals of sine, cosine, and tangent. They are the *cosecant*, defined as $\csc\theta = \frac{1}{\sin\theta}$, the *secant*, $\sec\theta = \frac{1}{\cos\theta}$, and the *cotangent*, $\cot\theta = \frac{1}{\tan\theta}$. Note that from the definition of tangent, $\cot\theta = \frac{\cos\theta}{\sin\theta}$.

In addition, there are three identities that relate the trigonometric functions to one another:

$$\cos\theta = \sin(\frac{\pi}{2} - \theta)$$

$$\csc\theta = \sec\left(\frac{\pi}{2} - \theta\right)$$

$$\cot\theta = \tan(\frac{\pi}{2} - \theta)$$

Here is a list of commonly-needed values for trigonometric functions, given in radians, for the first quadrant:

Table for trigonometric functions

$\sin 0 = 0$	$\cos 0 = 1$	$\tan 0 = 0$
$\sin\frac{\pi}{6} = \frac{1}{2}$	$\cos\frac{\pi}{6} = \frac{\sqrt{3}}{2}$	$\tan\frac{\pi}{6} = \frac{\sqrt{3}}{3}$
$\sin\frac{\pi}{4} = \frac{\sqrt{2}}{2}$	$\cos\frac{\pi}{4} = \frac{\sqrt{2}}{2}$	$\tan\frac{\pi}{4} = 1$
$\sin\frac{\pi}{3} = \frac{\sqrt{3}}{2}$	$\cos\frac{\pi}{3} = \frac{1}{2}$	$\tan\frac{\pi}{3} = \sqrt{3}$
$\sin\frac{\pi}{2} = 1$	$\cos\frac{\pi}{2} = 0$	$\tan\frac{\pi}{2} = \textit{undefined}$
$\csc 0 = \textit{undefined}$	$\sec 0 = 1$	$\cot 0 = \textit{undefined}$
$\csc\frac{\pi}{6} = 2$	$\sec\frac{\pi}{6} = \frac{2\sqrt{3}}{3}$	$\cot\frac{\pi}{6} = \sqrt{3}$
$\csc\frac{\pi}{4} = \sqrt{2}$	$\sec\frac{\pi}{4} = \sqrt{2}$	$\cot\frac{\pi}{4} = 1$
$\csc\frac{\pi}{3} = \frac{2\sqrt{3}}{3}$	$\sec\frac{\pi}{3} = 2$	$\cot\frac{\pi}{3} = \frac{\sqrt{3}}{3}$
$\csc\frac{\pi}{2} = 1$	$\sec\frac{\pi}{2} = \textit{undefined}$	$\cot\frac{\pi}{2} = 0$

To find the trigonometric values in other quadrants, complementary angles can be used. The *complementary angle* is the smallest angle between the *x*-axis and the given angle.

Once the complementary angle is known, the following rule is used:

For an angle θ with complementary angle x, the absolute value of a trigonometry function evaluated at θ is the same as the absolute value when evaluated at x.

The correct sign is used based on the functions sine and cosine are given by the *x* and *y* coordinates on the unit circle.

Sine will be positive in quadrants I and II and negative in quadrants III and IV.

Cosine will be positive in quadrants I and IV, and negative in II and III.

Tangent will be positive in I and III, and negative in II and IV.

The signs of the reciprocal functions will be the same as the sign of the function of which they are a reciprocal.

Example

Find $\sin\frac{3\pi}{4}$.

First, the complementary angle must be found.

This angle is in the II quadrant, and the angle between it and the *x*-axis is $\frac{\pi}{4}$.

Now, $\sin\frac{\pi}{4} = \frac{\sqrt{2}}{2}$.

Since this is in the II quadrant, sine takes on positive values (the *y* coordinate is positive in the II quadrant).

Therefore, $\sin\frac{3\pi}{4} = \frac{\sqrt{2}}{2}$.

In addition to the six trigonometric functions defined above, there are inverses for these functions. However, since the trigonometric functions are not one-to-one, one can only construct inverses for them on a restricted domain.

Usually, the domain chosen will be $[0,\pi)$ for cosine and $(-\frac{\pi}{2},\frac{\pi}{2}]$ for sine. The inverse for tangent can use either of these domains. The inverse functions for the trigonometric functions are also called *arc functions*. In addition to being written with a -1 in the exponent to denote that the function is an inverse, they will sometimes be written with an "a" or "arc" in front of the function name, so $\cos^{-1}\theta = \text{acos}\,\theta = \arccos\theta$.

When solving equations that involve trigonometric functions, there are often multiple solutions. For example, $2\sin\theta = \sqrt{2}$ can be simplified to $\sin\theta = \frac{\sqrt{2}}{2}$. This has solutions $\theta = \frac{\pi}{4}, \frac{3\pi}{4}$, but in addition, because of the periodicity, any integer multiple of 2π can also be added to these solutions to find another solution.

The full set of solutions is $\theta = \frac{\pi}{4} + 2\pi k, \frac{3\pi}{4} + 2\pi k$ for all integer values of *k*. It is very important to remember to find all possible solutions when dealing with equations that involve trigonometric functions.

The name *trigonometric* comes from the fact that these functions play an important role in the geometry of triangles, particularly right triangles.

Consider the right triangle shown in this figure:

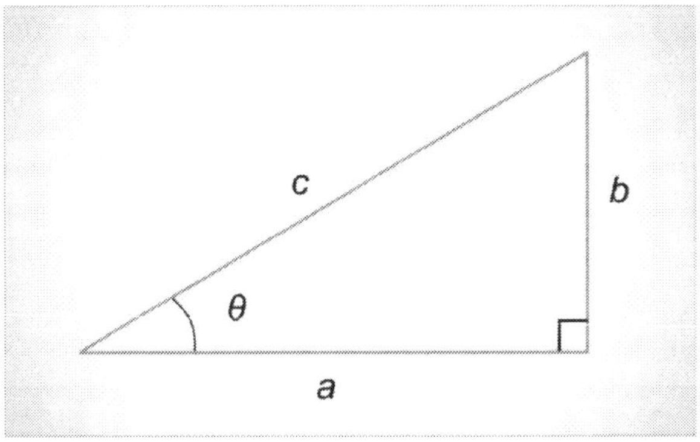

The following hold true:

- $c \sin\theta = b$
- $c \cos\theta = a$
- $\tan\theta = \frac{b}{a}$
- $b \csc\theta = c$
- $a \sec\theta = c$
- $\cot\theta = \frac{a}{b}$

Remember also the angles of a triangle must add up to π radians (180 degrees).

Practice Questions

1. Which of the following is the result of simplifying the expression:

$$\frac{4a^{-1}b^3}{a^4b^{-2}} * \frac{3a}{b}$$

a. $12a^3b^5$

b. $12\frac{b^4}{a^4}$

c. $\frac{12}{a^4}$

d. $7\frac{b^4}{a}$

2. The graph shows the position of a car over a 10-second time interval. Which of the following is the correct interpretation of the graph for the interval 1 to 3 seconds?

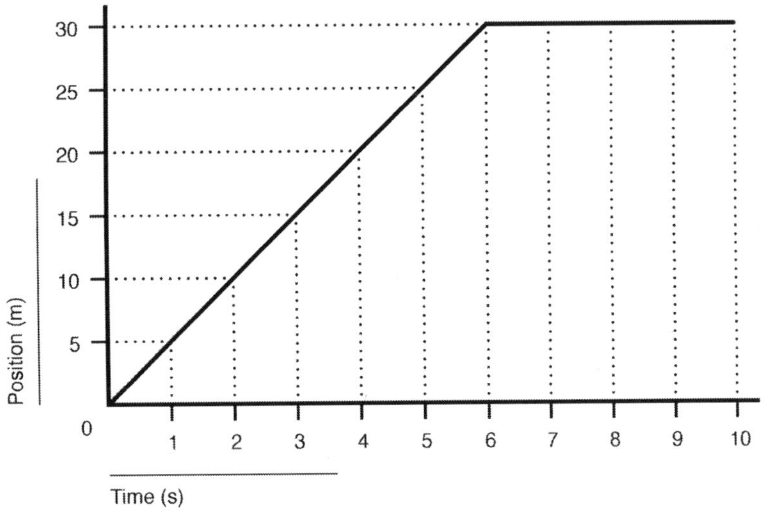

a. The car remains in the same position.
b. The car is traveling at a speed of 5m/s.
c. The car is traveling up a hill.
d. The car is traveling at 5mph.

3. What are the zeros of the function: $f(x) = x^3 + 4x^2 + 4x$?
a. -2
b. 0, -2
c. 2
d. 0, 2

4. If $g(x) = x^3 - 3x^2 - 2x + 6$ and $f(x) = 2$, then what is $g(f(x))$?
   a. -26
   b. 6
   c. $2x^3 - 6x^2 - 4x + 12$
   d. -2

5. Which of the following shows the correct result of simplifying the following expression:

$$(7n + 3n^3 + 3) + (8n + 5n^3 + 2n^4)$$

   a. $9n^4 + 15n - 2$
   b. $2n^4 + 5n^3 + 15n - 2$
   c. $9n^4 + 8n^3 + 15n$
   d. $2n^4 + 8n^3 + 15n + 3$

6. What is the product of the following expression?

$$(4x - 8)(5x^2 + x + 6)$$

   a. $20x^3 - 36x^2 + 16x - 48$
   b. $6x^3 - 41x^2 + 12x + 15$
   c. $204 + 11x^2 - 37x - 12$
   d. $2x^3 - 11x^2 - 32x + 20$

7. How could the following equation be factored to find the zeros?

$$y = x^3 - 3x^2 - 4x$$

   a. $0 = x^2(x - 4), x = 0, 4$
   b. $0 = 3x(x + 1)(x + 4), x = 0, -1, -4$
   c. $0 = x(x + 1)(x + 6), x = 0, -1, -6$
   d. $0 = x(x + 1)(x - 4), x = 0, -1, 4$

8. What is the simplified quotient of the following expression?

$$\frac{5x^3}{3x^2y} \div \frac{25}{3y^9}$$

   a. $\frac{125x}{9y^{10}}$
   b. $\frac{x}{5y^8}$
   c. $\frac{5}{xy^8}$
   d. $\frac{xy^8}{5}$

9. What is the solution for the following equation?

$$\frac{x^2 + x - 30}{x - 5} = 11$$

a. $x = -6$
b. There is no solution.
c. $x = 16$
d. $x = 5$

10. What is the function that forms an equivalent graph to $y = \cos(x)$?
a. $y = \tan(x)$
b. $y = \csc(x)$
c. $y = \sin(x + \frac{\pi}{2})$
d. $y = \sin(x - \frac{\pi}{2})$

11. What is the solution for the equation $\tan(x) + 1 = 0$, where $0 \leq x < 2\pi$?
a. $x = \frac{3\pi}{4}, \frac{5\pi}{4}$

b. $x = \frac{3\pi}{4}, \frac{\pi}{4}$

c. $x = \frac{5\pi}{4}, \frac{7\pi}{4}$

d. $x = \frac{3\pi}{4}, \frac{7\pi}{4}$

12. What is the inverse of the function $f(x) = 3x - 5$?
a. $f^{-1}(x) = \frac{x}{3} + 5$
b. $f^{-1}(x) = \frac{5x}{3}$
c. $f^{-1}(x) = 3x + 5$
d. $f^{-1}(x) = \frac{x+5}{3}$

13. What are the zeros of $f(x) = x^2 + 4$?
a. $x = -4$
b. $x = \pm 2i$
c. $x = \pm 2$
d. $x = \pm 4i$

14. What are the y-intercept(s) for $y = x^2 + 3x - 4$?
a. $y = 1$
b. $y = -4$
c. $y = 3$
d. $y = 4$

15. Is the following function even, odd, neither, or both?

$$y = \frac{1}{2}x^4 + 2x^2 - 6$$

a. Even
b. Odd
c. Neither
d. Both

16. Which equation is not a function?
a. $y = |x|$
b. $y = \sqrt{x}$
c. $x = 3$
d. $y = 4$

17. How could the following function be rewritten to identify the zeros?

$$y = 3x^3 + 3x^2 - 18x$$

a. $y = 3x(x + 3)(x - 2)$
b. $y = x(x - 2)(x + 3)$
c. $y = 3x(x - 3)(x + 2)$
d. $y = (x + 3)(x - 2)$

18. What is the slope of the line tangent to the graph of $y = x^3 - 4$ at the point where $x = 2$?
a. $3x^2$
b. 4
c. -4
d. 12

19. What is the answer to $(2 + 2i)(2 - 2i)$?
a. 8
b. 8*i*
c. 4
d. 4*i*

20. What is the answer to $\frac{2+2i}{2-2i}$?
a. 8
b. 8*i*
c. 2*i*
d. *i*

Answer Explanations

1. B: To simplify the given equation, the first step is to make all exponents positive by moving them to the opposite place in the fraction. This expression becomes:

$$\frac{4b^3b^2}{a^1a^4} * \frac{3a}{b}$$

Then the rules for exponents can be used to simplify. Multiplying the same bases means the exponents can be added. Dividing the same bases means the exponents are subtracted.

2. B: The car is traveling at a speed of five meters per second. On the interval from one to three seconds, the position changes by fifteen meters. By making this change in position over time into a rate, the speed becomes ten meters in two seconds or five meters in one second.

3. B: There are two zeros for the given function. They are $x = 0, -2$. The zeros can be found a number of ways, but this particular equation can be factored into:

$$f(x) = x(x^2 + 4x + 4) = x(x + 2)(x + 2)$$

By setting each factor equal to zero and solving for x, there are two solutions. On a graph, these zeros can be seen where the line crosses the x-axis.

4. D: This problem involves a composition function, where one function is plugged into the other function. In this case, the $f(x)$ function is plugged into the $g(x)$ function for each x-value. The composition equation becomes:

$$g(f(x)) = 2^3 - 3(2^2) - 2(2) + 6$$

Simplifying the equation gives the answer:

$$g(f(x)) = 8 - 3(4) - 2(2) + 6 = 8 - 12 - 4 + 6 = -2$$

5. D: The expression is simplified by collecting like terms. Terms with the same variable and exponent are like terms, and their coefficients can be added.

6. A: Finding the product means distributing one polynomial to the other so that each term in the first is multiplied by each term in the second. Then, like terms can be collected. Multiplying the factors yields the expression:

$$20x^3 + 4x^2 + 24x - 40x^2 - 8x - 48$$

Collecting like terms means adding the x^2 terms and adding the x terms. The final answer after simplifying the expression is:

$$20x^3 - 36x^2 + 16x - 48$$

7. D: Finding the zeros for a function by factoring is done by setting the equation equal to zero, then completely factoring. Since there was a common x for each term in the provided equation, that is factored out first. Then the quadratic that is left can be factored into two binomials: $(x + 1)(x - 4)$. Setting each factor equation equal to zero and solving for x yields three zeros.

8. D: Dividing rational expressions follows the same rule as dividing fractions. The division is changed to multiplication, and the reciprocal is found in the second fraction. This turns the expression into:

$$\frac{5x^3}{3x^2} * \frac{3y^9}{25}$$

Multiplying across and simplifying, the final expression is:

$$\frac{xy^8}{5}$$

9. B: The equation can be solved by factoring the numerator into $(x + 6)(x - 5)$. Since that same factor $(x - 5)$ exists on top and bottom, that factor cancels. This leaves the equation $x + 6 = 11$. Solving the equation gives the answer $x = 5$. When this value is plugged into the equation, it yields a zero in the denominator of the fraction. Since this is undefined, there is no solution.

10. C: Graphing the function $y = \cos(x)$ shows that the curve starts at $(0, 1)$, has an amplitude of 2, and a period of 2π. This same curve can be constructed using the sine graph, by shifting the graph to the left $\frac{\pi}{2}$ units. This equation is in the form $y = \sin(x + \frac{\pi}{2})$.

11. D: Using SOHCAHTOA, tangent is $\frac{y}{x}$ for the special triangles. Since the value needs to be negative one, the angle must be some form of 45 degrees or $\frac{\pi}{4}$. The value is negative in the second and fourth quadrant, so the answer is $\frac{3\pi}{4}$ and $\frac{7\pi}{4}$.

12. D: The inverse of a function is found by following these steps:

1. Change f(x) to y.
2. Switch the x and y in the equation.
3. Solve for y. In the given equation, solving for y is done by adding 5 to both sides, then dividing both sides by 3.

This answer can be checked on the graph by verifying the lines are reflected over $y = x$.

13. B: The zeros of this function can be found by using the quadratic formula:

$$x = \frac{-b \pm \sqrt{b^2 - 4ac}}{2a}$$

Identifying *a*, *b*, and *c* can be done from the equation as well because it is in standard form. The formula becomes:

$$x = \frac{0 \pm \sqrt{0^2 - 4(1)(4)}}{2(1)} = \frac{\sqrt{-16}}{2}$$

Since there is a negative underneath the radical, the answer is a complex number.

14. B: The y-intercept of an equation is found where the x -value is zero. Plugging zero into the equation for x, the first two terms cancel out, leaving -4.

15. A: The equation is *even* because $f(-x) = f(x)$. Plugging in a negative value will result in the same answer as when plugging in the positive of that same value. The function:

$$f(-2) = \frac{1}{2}(-2)^4 + 2(-2)^2 - 6 = 8 + 8 - 6 = 10$$

yields the same value as:

$$f(2) = \frac{1}{2}(2)^4 + 2(2)^2 - 6 = 8 + 8 - 6 = 10$$

16. C: The equation $x = 3$ is not a function because it does not pass the vertical line test. This test is made from the definition of a function, where each x-value must be mapped to one and only one y-value. This equation is a vertical line, so the x-value of 3 is mapped with an infinite number of y-values.

17. A: The function can be factored to identify the zeros. First, the term $3x$ is factored out to the front because each term contains $3x$. Then, the quadratic is factored into $(x + 3)(x - 2)$.

18. D: Finding the slope of the line tangent to the given function involves taking the derivative twice. The first derivative gives the line tangent to the graph. The second derivative finds the slope of that line. The line tangent to the graph has an equation $y' = 3x^2$. The slope of this line at $x = 2$ is found by the second derivative, y = 6x, or $y = 6(2) = 12$.

19. A: This answer is correct because $(2 + 2i)(2 - 2i)$, using the FOIL method is:

$$4 - 4i + 4i - 4i^2 = 8$$

Choice *B* is not the answer because there is no *i* in the final answer, since the *i*'s cancel out in the FOIL. Choice *C*, 4, is not the final answer because we add $4 + 4$ in the end to equal 8. Choice *D*, 4*i*, is not the final answer because there is neither a 4 nor an *i* in the final answer.

20. D: Multiply the top and the bottom by $(2 + 2i)$, the conjugate, to arrive at $\frac{8i}{8}$, which cancels to *i*. Choice *A* is not the answer because the 8's cancel out. Choice *B* is not the answer because the 8's cancel out. Choice *C* is not the answer because 2 is not left, but 8 is.

Dear Next-Generation ACCUPLACER Test Taker,

We would like to start by thanking you for purchasing this study guide for your Next-Generation ACCUPLACER exam. We hope that we exceeded your expectations.

Our goal in creating this study guide was to cover all of the topics that you will see on the test. We also strove to make our practice questions as similar as possible to what you will encounter on test day. With that being said, if you found something that you feel was not up to your standards, please send us an email and let us know.

We would also like to let you know about other books in our catalog that may interest you.

TSI

This can be found on Amazon: amazon.com/dp/162845511X

SAT

amazon.com/dp/1628454679

ACT

amazon.com/dp/1628454709

SAT Math 1

amazon.com/dp/1628454717

AP Biology

amazon.com/dp/1628454989

We have study guides in a wide variety of fields. If the one you are looking for isn't listed above, then try searching for it on Amazon or send us an email.

Thanks Again and Happy Testing!
Product Development Team
info@studyguideteam.com

FREE Test Taking Tips DVD Offer

To help us better serve you, we have developed a Test Taking Tips DVD that we would like to give you for FREE. **This DVD covers world-class test taking tips that you can use to be even more successful when you are taking your test.**

All that we ask is that you email us your feedback about your study guide. Please let us know what you thought about it – whether that is good, bad or indifferent.

To get your **FREE Test Taking Tips DVD**, email freedvd@studyguideteam.com with "FREE DVD" in the subject line and the following information in the body of the email:

a. The title of your study guide.
b. Your product rating on a scale of 1-5, with 5 being the highest rating.
c. Your feedback about the study guide. What did you think of it?
d. Your full name and shipping address to send your free DVD.

If you have any questions or concerns, please don't hesitate to contact us at freedvd@studyguideteam.com.

Thanks again!

21857321R00098

Made in the USA
Columbia, SC
21 July 2018